WAITING FOR A
MIRACLE
ONE MOTHER'S JOURNEY TO UNSHAKABLE FAITH

Julie.

Listen to Mary —
She leads us all to her
Son. Jesus!

Blessings,
Cyndi Peterson

CYNDI PETERSON, MD
WITH GINGER KOLBABA

A SAVIO REPUBLIC BOOK

ISBN: 978-1-68261-139-5
ISBN (eBook): 978-1-68261-140-1

WAITING FOR A MIRACLE
One Mother's Journey to Unshakable Faith
© 2016 by Cyndi Peterson with Ginger Kolbaba
All Rights Reserved

Cover Design by Christian Bentulan

SAVIO
REPVBLIC

To my husband Drew, and our sons Drew Jr, Johnny, and Jack, whose support and love have been endless and to my mother, Margie, who constantly modeled her trust in God to all of her children.

CONTENTS

Author's Note --- ix

Foreword -- xi

Chapter 1: Pleading for a Miracle ------------------------------------- 1

Part 1
A Call to Faith

Chapter 2: Everything I Wanted ------------------------------------- 8

Chapter 3: The Dream -- 13

Chapter 4: Hiding --- 17

Chapter 5: "It's My Brother's Fault" ----------------------------- 26

Chapter 6: Signs and Wonders -------------------------------------- 35

Chapter 7: The Admission-- 44

Part 2
Medjugorje

Chapter 8: The First Night --- 48

Chapter 9: Making a Deal with God ----------------------------- 57

Chapter 10: More Signs --61

Part 3
Kelly

Chapter 11: It's a Girl!--- 76
Chapter 12: Searching for Answers ----------------------------------- 84
Chapter 13: The Diagnosis-- 93
Chapter 14: Time to Confess --- 100
Chapter 15: Back to Medjugorje-------------------------------------- 109
Chapter 16: A Call to Obedience------------------------------------- 118
Chapter 17: More Desperate Prayers -------------------------------- 131
Chapter 18: A Tough Surrender-------------------------------------- 141
Chapter 19: Another Child? -- 149
Chapter 20: The Deepest Pain --------------------------------------- 157
Chapter 21: The Funeral --- 160

Part 4
Sarah

Chapter 22: "We Can Help You" ------------------------------------- 168
Chapter 23: A Healthy Baby Girl!----------------------------------- 177
Chapter 24: Blindsided -- 182
Chapter 25: Return to Medjugorje---------------------------------- 190
Chapter 26: Enjoying Sarah -- 194
Chapter 27: Questions for God -------------------------------------- 199
Chapter 28: Another Funeral --205
Chapter 29: A Mother's Vision--------------------------------------- 212
Chapter 30: Discovering the Miracles------------------------------- 215

Appendix A: Reflections on *Waiting for a Miracle* ------------- 221
Appendix B: Medjugorje--- 234
Acknowledgments -- 237
About the Authors -- 241

AUTHOR'S NOTE

When people hear bits of my story, they tell me they think, *Wow, that's depressing. She lost two daughters? And worse, she got pregnant with one child when she was burying another— knowing that the baby growing in her womb could die too? What kind of crazy woman does that?*

But then when they hear the whole story—the rawness, the vulnerability, the determination, the redemption, and the joy that ultimately came from the entire experience, they say, "I want to know that joy. If God was present with her and gave her strength and peace, then he can do the same for me."

Every one of us has pain in our lives, but the question is: what do I do with my pain? We always hear, "Turn to God," but what does that involve? My story illustrates a real-life person of average faith, confronted with tragedy beyond imagination, who does turn to God, and in the end is better for it.

Pain will enter our lives with or without God. I trust my story will inspire you to take your sorrow and risk going to God with it to discover that he does not abandon us in our need. He truly desires to redeem our suffering, to do miraculous things with our inevitable pain, and in the end, transform it and ourselves into the miraculous. There is triumph from the cross available to us all.

FOREWORD

In *Waiting for a Miracle*, Cyndi Peterson has accomplished what thousands of first-time writers can only dream of doing—that is write a story that grabs the reader from the opening paragraph to the last line in the final chapter. It is a rare achievement made even more special because it is a story of deep, anguish-filled suffering that miraculously brings about the deepest of spiritual conversions.

Many manuscripts penned by souls dramatically touched by the ongoing daily apparitions of the Blessed Virgin Mary at the tiny village of Medjugorje in Bosnia-Hercegovina, are sent to my office. The would-be authors usually ask for an opinion on how good their story is followed by would I help them get it published? The vast majority of the manuscripts are returned to the sender with a note of encouragement. Such witness and the desire to tell their own story by those who have been to Medjugorje gives added credence to its continuous good spiritual fruits.

However, there is more to the story of how this witness by Cyndi developed into the writing of *Waiting for a Miracle*.

Cyndi had actually sent her original manuscript to me several years ago, asking if I might be interested in helping her get the story published. I glanced at it at the time and was mildly interested but too involved with other writing projects to pay proper attention to it. Then in the summer of 2015, I received a well-ordered, revised outline of Cyndi's manuscript with a professionally planned overview and succinct samples from each proposed chapter of her manuscript. I was duly impressed; yet, again too busy locked into an intense writing schedule to meet the deadline of my next book. Once again Cyndi's manuscript was placed on my desk in the stack of material to be read later. It stayed there unopened and unread.

Part of the travel agenda consuming most of my time was an annual November pilgrimage to the apparition site of Medjugorje. As always, I had a full schedule of speaking to other pilgrimage groups while there. It was a packed speaking schedule that would fill most of my time during the tour.

On the last full day in Medjugorje, I spoke to a group of pilgrims mainly from California. It turned out to be a pilgrimage led by Cyndi.

After the talk Cyndi approached me and asked if I had read her manuscript she had sent to my office. I had to confess somewhat embarrassed, that I had not. But, I promised her, I would read it immediately on my return home. That was fine, she responded with a quiet determination, but she had the manuscript on her computer, which she had brought with her on the pilgrimage. She would be glad to send it to me right then and there so I could read it during the flight home. Fine, I said with grudging admiration of her tenacity, send it to me.

I began reading Cyndi's manuscript before leaving Medjugorje, more out of curiosity and admiration of her tenacity than anything else; plus I felt guilty that I had not even bothered to read what she had sent me.

Within the first two chapters of the manuscript, I knew it had to be published. It was as if Jesus was looking over my shoulder and telling me to read more and I would understand.

By the time my plane landed in Atlanta, I had completed the entire manuscript. On arriving home I began to edit and suggest subtle changes despite the jet lag. I wanted to meet with this woman immediately and learn more.

The question was, how would I find time to meet with Cyndi? I would be home for only three days before heading to California and then on to Seattle, Washington for talks. After that trip it was home again for four days and then off to Africa for ten days. Still, I had to call her to see if we could meet at some point in the near future.

Cyndi was pleased that I had read her manuscript and, I think, somewhat surprised at my enthusiasm and desire that we meet to discuss the details. By the way, I asked her, where do you live? Just outside of San Diego, California, she told me. Of course. I suddenly remembered that her Medjugorje pilgrimage group was from California.

I would be staying in Brea during my California trip, so I asked Cyndi how far was that from her home. Just about an hour and a half, she responded. Within a few minutes we arranged to meet in Brea the next day. I was beginning to feel that special Holy Spirit presence that always comes when heaven wants to accomplish something unusual. Closing my phone I smiled as I thought of a saying I used so often in my talks: With God, there are no coincidences!

After three hours of working together and going over the manuscript, there was no doubt that this book needed to be published—and soon. I could just feel Our Lady's fingerprints all over the entire set of unusual circumstances that brought us together. But then again, there are no coincidences with God; everything is by plan and design. As you read Cyndi's story you will understand why Heaven wanted it published.

- Wayne Weible

CHAPTER 1

Pleading for a Miracle

I clutched my five-month-old daughter, Kelly, willing her to breathe. Every few minutes I suctioned out her nostrils and throat. But she fought me, fussy, gasping for breath, half-whining, half-crying.

This is crazy, I thought frantically. *She's supposed to get better here, not worse.*

"Come on, Kelly. Come on, sweetie." How could I explain to a five month old that if she calmed down, things would seem better? The irony wasn't lost on me. *Calm down.* I felt as much a wreck as she was.

I spied a drinking fountain off to the side of the courtyard where we waited to see Father Jozo and remembered that Kelly hadn't eaten in a while. Maybe if I could get her to eat something, that would calm her down and she would feel better. I gently placed Kelly back into her stroller, grabbed the formula and a bottle from her baby bag, and headed to the fountain.

I gripped the nozzle and gave it a twist. Nothing. The bottom of the fountain was bone dry. I twisted again harder. It had to work. Kelly's tortured, gasping whimpers were constant now. I clinched my fist—an outward symbol of what my chest was doing. What my soul was doing.

My husband, Drew, came to the fountain to help.

"It's... it's *not* working!" I felt so frustrated, so helpless. I had been a military doctor—I had seen everything the medical and military communities could throw at me—from rare diseases to catastrophes. I'd been calm and rational in every circumstance. When a volcano erupted on the island where I was stationed and thick ash covered my base—I'd handled it with strength and poise. When a fellow soldier from my squadron was killed in a helicopter accident and his remains burned beyond recognition, I kept a cool head and did my job.

This was different. This was *my child*. My baby girl. Drew and I had prayed for a girl. We'd pinned our hopes and dreams on this precious gift.

"She's struggling!" I looked desperately around the courtyard for another fountain. "I'm going to go find some water." Still grasping the bottle, I ran toward the church. I stepped into the dimly lit foyer at the back by the sacristy—the room where the priests' vestments are kept—and could hear Father Jozo giving his homily on how we must trust God, that he knows our every need. Right then I needed water. I rushed down a hallway to my left but could find nothing. I could no longer catch my breath.

My thoughts became frantic. *This isn't how it's supposed to happen. We're supposed to bring her on this trip. We're following*

God's plan. I knew enough from my medical training that Kelly could die. But we still had at least another four months. Four months.

She could die at the place where she's supposed to be healed.

I turned and headed the other way. My hand had grown sweaty around the bottle.

What do I do? I don't know how to help her! My mind swirled until it began to doubt. *Should we have even brought her here? Should we just go home?*

But we'd traveled halfway around the world. We'd come to Medjugorje, the place of miracles, because I'd received miracles here before. Now my daughter needed a miracle.

I'd prayed. I'd begged God to heal her. Everyone I knew was doing the same. And my heart kept nudging me back to this place. To Father Jozo, a man strong in the Spirit. A holy man who, with one touch and one prayer, could restore health and bring wholeness. *I knew* Kelly would be okay if we could just get her to him. But we were running out of time. And he was still speaking, no urgency in his voice, no comprehension that he needed to hurry things along.

I have to get her formula! my mind screamed. A part of me— the rational part—knew the formula wasn't going to do much to help my daughter. My quest seemed wild and inexplicable. But it was the only thing I could control. I could find water. I could make formula for her to drink. I would do that, if nothing else.

I stopped and gasped a tiny cry. A door to my side opened and a nun stepped out and looked at me. Her face registered concern, and in a language I couldn't understand she asked me something.

"Water. I need water!" I held up the bottle and tried to communicate through sign language. My eyes were moist with tears.

Finally, she understood and nodded. Lifting a hand, she gestured for me to follow her down the hall. On her heels, I shadowed her until she opened another door and pointed inside. There was a drinking fountain.

"Thank you!" I said, running to the fountain, half afraid it wasn't going to work either. As I turned the nozzle, fresh, cold water flowed out and splashed onto the base. I filled the bottle and rushed back to the courtyard. As soon as I opened the church door, I saw Drew hunched over Kelly, suctioning out the secretions. He looked hopefully toward me. I grabbed the formula, poured it into the bottle, and picked up Kelly to feed her. Her little body felt so limp in my arms, it was like holding a rag doll.

Now she'll be okay, I reassured myself.

Clear, runny secretions kept oozing from her nostrils. I suctioned it out again and put the bottle to Kelly's lips. Since she had little muscle tone, she was unable to turn her head away, but still she wouldn't allow me to feed her.

"She can't breathe, that's why she won't eat." Drew, also a doctor, said what we both knew. I looked at him pleadingly. Now tears gathered on my eyelashes. I blinked hard, trying to keep them at bay. I wouldn't cry. The rational part of me knew it would do no good right now. But my heart felt otherwise.

"What are we going to do?" I asked, hoping he'd have the answer, but knowing he wouldn't. He was as helpless as I was. Without saying it, we refused to take her to the local hospital.

I suctioned her again, held her up against my chest, and patted her back. Nothing helped.

My dreaded reality crashed down like a boulder onto my heart. *She's going to die. Right here in my arms, before we can even get her to see the priest. Why, God? I did everything you asked. I brought her all the way over here. I did as much as I could. There's nothing left for me to do.*

And God wasn't coming through. I felt lost. I looked at my precious daughter suffering, and I couldn't fathom that God wouldn't heal her. Why wouldn't he heal a beautiful little girl with parents who had faith, who were sharing their faith, who were willing to be ridiculed as physicians for taking their daughter halfway around the world in search of a miracle? That alone was playing a fool for God in the medical world.

We did it all and where was God? He had the power. And Kelly was an innocent little life. What possible reason would there be for her to die?

I suctioned her again and gently nudged the bottle against her lips. She was spent and felt listless in my arms. Her eyes were sorrowful and held deep anguish. And her face bore a light shade of blue. I looked again at Drew. All the color had drained from his face.

PART 1

A Call to Faith

CHAPTER 2

Everything I Wanted

I never really wanted to be married. I hate to admit that I never really wanted to be a mom. And if I'm honest, faith wasn't really high on my priority list either.

I had my eyes set on something else: from the time I was twelve I wanted to be a doctor. I loved everything about the medical field. I loved science, helping people, and being in control. I loved the challenge of figuring out diseases and how the body worked. I loved that I could be an expert in a specific area of medicine. And I knew that becoming a physician meant long hours, a fast pace, and a heavy workload—all things that don't leave room for a family. But my independent streak made me okay with that trade-off. Solving the mysteries of science would give me all the fulfillment I wanted or needed.

Although I was raised Catholic, religion didn't hold my interest either, and it certainly didn't seem to connect to science. Growing up I attended parochial school where we were taught that God is love. But that didn't mean a whole lot. I had no use for a faith that gave me little guidance but wanted me to give up control to a God who loved me but who didn't seem all that powerful or interested in my daily life. And even though I attended a Catholic college and medical school, I learned more to trust my own instincts, that science and medicine would ultimately cure or handle any problem, and I could control my own destiny. So while I attended mass most weeks, it was more out of guilt. It really had no meaning, and other than mass, faith never entered my life outside of one hour a week.

I studied hard and made it through college with my dream intact. But at the end of my first year of medical school, I ran out of funds, and in order to continue, I joined the navy. Under their health professional scholarship program, the navy paid all my medical school expenses in exchange for four years of service. It meant putting off a residency in dermatology—my desired field— but it offered an opportunity to put my medical skills to use in other ways. Although I'd never considered a life in the military, at a loss for other financial options, I knew this was the route to help me realize my goal. So I accepted, was commissioned as a lieutenant in the United States Navy, completed medical school, and headed to San Diego for my new life to begin.

Everything was going according to plan and I enjoyed every minute of my service. The navy ended up being a wonderful adventure in which I gained essential medical experience, I made friends, and loved the life of being a navy officer.

Then I met Drew and my whole life changed.

Drew was an orthopedic doctor who was also serving in the military. I was immediately attracted to him, but still wasn't interested in getting involved since I had my military service and then my residency to consider. But as we dated, I felt my goals begin to shift. Perhaps I could make room in my career for a husband—especially since Drew had become my best friend. I could tell him anything and we could talk for hours. He was handsome and one of the kindest men I'd met. And I fell in love.

And when he proposed I immediately said yes.

We married and Drew wanted to start a family. Again I was faced with possibly compromising my dream. Could I obtain the career I'd worked so hard for *and* be a mother? I had my doubts, but agreed to have children.

When I got pregnant and then suffered a miscarriage at eight weeks, I was surprised by how devastated I was. I hadn't really wanted children, but then to mourn the very thing I'd thought I didn't want came as a shock. And worse was how I found out.

I went to my doctor for an ultrasound and as the radiologist was running the test, he blurted out, "Well, there's no heartbeat. That baby's definitely not going to make it." I was crushed, and I could barely get out of the office. I ran into the bathroom and sobbed.

With that pregnancy, I'd found myself with all these emotions and dreams of the way life would be with this baby. And in a blink it was gone. The baby. The dreams. I mourned for months.

Slowly life returned to normal and I continued down my career path. And soon I was pregnant again and gave birth to our son, Drew Jr. I found that I treasured this precious child and was astonished that I loved being needed—and wanted. I began to cherish this idea of motherhood and didn't argue when Drew wanted us to try for another child.

But eight weeks into this new pregnancy, miscarriage visited me again. I couldn't understand why. I knew that I could get pregnant and give birth to a healthy child, so why was I forced to suffer another miscarriage? For some reason, though I mourned, this loss didn't hit me as hard as the first one. Perhaps because I was busy with my career and my toddler.

Two years later, along came John.

I worked hard to balance my work and family. I continued my time in the navy and pursued my residency in dermatology there. But soon I discovered my goals began to change again. While I still wanted to be a specialist in my field, I now wondered about my military time—I worried about being deployed and away from my family. So after nine years with the navy, now as a Lt. Commander, I made the difficult decision to leave. I hadn't dreamed of being in the military, but I enjoyed my time and service, and I loved all the people I had worked with. It had become an integral part of me.

I went on to complete a fellowship in Mohs Micrographic Surgery at Scripps Clinic in La Jolla, California. Mohs surgery is a special tissue-sparing method of removing skin cancers. It was an extremely busy year, and I reveled in every minute of it.

But another change came at the end of my fellowship year when I gave birth to our third child, Jack. I found parenting a family of three was the most difficult thing I had ever done. To handle three small boys at once was no easy task. So I transitioned into private practice, which allowed me more time to spend with my family.

I had worked hard to succeed and now I had everything I had ever wanted: a fulfilling career, a wonderful husband, three adorable and active boys, and a beautiful home overlooking the Pacific Ocean (that had even been featured in *Better Homes and Gardens*). My life was complete. I could think of nothing else I desired.

CHAPTER 3

The Dream

I stood in an enormous house with raised ceilings and open, spacious rooms. It was a beautiful and comfortable home, uncluttered and well kept, with well-placed furniture and decorations throughout. A large floral arrangement graced the round entry table, and as I glanced around the house I noticed several smaller bouquets. I went to the second floor and began to look around, locating every closet, every chest, any nook and cranny. I saw a large desk in one of the rooms and I walked to it. One by one, I pulled open the drawers and rummaged through the contents. I couldn't find what I was looking for.

My search became more desperate as I headed to a large side table, pulled open the drawers, and spilled the contents on the floor.

Where is it? I wondered.

I walked quickly to the adjoining room, threw open a closet door, and began pushing clothes out of my way. I reached onto the top shelves and grabbed the boxes there. An intense drive within me compelled me to keep looking. But it wasn't there either. In frustration I began to pull out the clothes and throw them to the floor. I was growing more frantic in my search.

Suddenly, as I grabbed more clothes to push out of the way, I heard a soft, penetrating voice from overhead.

"Cyndi, what are you doing?"

"I'm looking for something," I said, still throwing anything that was in my way.

"What are you looking for?"

"I'm looking for something!"

"What?"

I fell to my knees with a heavy sigh, still clutching the clothes I had in my hands. I took a deep breath and answered. "That's just it. I have absolutely no idea. But I can't stop looking!"

I dropped my head to my chest in utter frustration.

In that moment of silence, the voice said, "You are looking for the meaning of your life. And your search will lead you straight into the arms of Jesus."

I awoke with a start, the vivid dream still seared in my mind. My heart was pounding against my chest and I was breathing rapidly.

I lay listening to my surroundings, partially paralyzed from fear. Finally I gathered my courage to look at Drew, who was sleeping comfortably next to me.

What in the world does Jesus have to do with anything? I wondered. I hadn't thought about Jesus in so long that it felt strange even to hear his name. Other than the times my family and I attended mass, Jesus never entered my thoughts. And to be honest, Jesus rarely entered my mind during mass either.

I mentally replayed the dream. I tried to think of something that may have triggered it, since experts say our subconscious often deals with the issues from our daily life. But there was nothing. I wasn't experiencing any trauma or feeling any pull toward God. My life was perfect. I had everything I wanted or needed. I was happy. I was successful.

So why was I so desperate in my search?

I rolled over and pulled the covers up around my neck. A small thought began to nag at the back of my mind: *Am I really happy? Is my life really complete?* Without acknowledging it, I knew the answer.

No.

With the wealth and success and family and career, happiness always seemed to elude me, as though it were just beyond my grasp. It wasn't that I was unhappy; I just wasn't completely satisfied. For years I'd felt that something was missing. I remembered getting my diploma from medical school and thinking that would make me feel I'd achieved everything and I would have this unbelievable sense of accomplishment and completeness. I thought I was going to be like, *I achieved that. I'm a doctor!* But I felt exactly the same as I did the day before.

I figured it would come after I finished my internship—*then* I'd feel complete. But it didn't happen then either. So I thought that if I could get accepted into dermatology, I would feel whole.

At one point I'd considered going to law school, to get a dual degree, because I thought maybe I just needed another degree. And then I figured, well, maybe when I got married, then I would be... but no.

Birth of my first child. No.

With each new accomplishment I had thought, *Now I'll be fulfilled.* I had achieved awesome things! But a peace and centeredness never quite settled completely over me.

What you're looking for is Jesus.

No, that couldn't be it. After all, I'd spent years in Catholic school. My mom was a devout Catholic. My uncle was a priest and my aunt a nun. I'd tried the religious route. And three decades of church and spirituality hadn't succeeded in fulfilling me.

What you're looking for is the meaning of your life, and your search will drive you into the arms of Jesus.

Jesus! How ridiculous. How absurd. But I couldn't push it out of my mind—the dream seemed so real.

It's just a dream, I finally concluded. *It doesn't mean anything.* But as I closed my eyes and drifted back to sleep, I still wondered if there were some clues there. And how exactly *could* Jesus fit into my life's purpose?

CHAPTER 4

Hiding

*J*esus. I was so far from Jesus. And I felt sad that I wasn't exposing my children as much as I should to a relationship with Christ, even though they were just babies.

I wanted to get closer to Christ. I hadn't realized how far I had drifted from my faith. But I wasn't ready to take any major steps to get back to my Catholic roots—other than attending mass. Drew had never expressed much interest in spiritual things and I didn't really want to broach the topic with him, so I kept it to myself.

Three months after the dream, one afternoon I left work at the usual time and headed home. I pulled onto El Camino Real and drove through the heart of Encinitas. The traffic, which was usually heavy at that time of day, was like a parking lot. I hit stoplight after stoplight, and the six-mile trip from my office building to my house seemed to take forever. Twenty minutes passed and I was still sitting in the jam and growing frustrated.

As I hit yet another stoplight, I sighed heavily and began mindlessly to look at the shopping center to my right. I spotted the usual places—Rubio's Fish Tacos, T J Maxx, and a cinema. Then one store in particular caught my eye. The sign above the shop said "Chronicles" and another sign in the window announced that this was a Christian bookstore. I'd never seen that store before. I'd made that drive at least a year-and-a-half and had never noticed it.

I remembered that my niece's baptism was the following weekend and I needed to get her a gift.

Maybe they'll have something appropriate in there, I thought. I glanced around at the thick traffic and then looked at my watch. It was getting late and I needed to get home to start making dinner. But I was still a good distance from the house and I really didn't want just to sit in my car.

So I wormed my way toward the parking lot entrance, made a quick right-hand turn, and parked. As I stepped out of my car, I started to rethink my decision. I'd never before been in a Christian bookstore. I wasn't sure what to expect and felt nervous about what I might experience. I knew they weren't going to attack me! But I had an odd feeling about the whole prospect of entering this new and unknown world.

I knew I didn't have a lot of time, so that helped calm me. I'd rush in, take a quick look around, hopefully find something, buy it, and get out. So I picked up my step and headed for the door.

As soon as I walked in I felt overwhelmed. There was a lot to take in all at once! Christian stuff was everywhere. I noticed a sweet, pleasant aroma that permeated the shop. Some type of contemporary music filtered through a speaker system. I was surprised that the music was kind of catchy. Not the hymns I would have imagined, but more contemporary. The singers talked about how God loves us.

A tall woman approached me, smiling. She looked to be in her fifties, medium build, with short brown hair and reading glasses, and as-sweet-as-pie nice. For some reason, the whole scene irritated me. Everything about the shop felt syrupy and sappy.

"Can I help you?" she asked.

"No, no. It's okay. I'll just look." I felt uneasy and definitely out of my element. I wanted to "blend in" as if I felt completely at ease, but I wasn't sure what exactly I was looking for, so I decided just to roam. The store was brimming with every kind of religious item I could have imagined. I walked past a counter that looked like a jewelry case. It held rings and bracelets and bookmarks, and on the top were placed little keychain ornaments. To my left was a whole section of CDs and DVDs. Another section had rows of books, and the back wall housed a whole row of Bibles. Throughout the store were banners and artwork hanging from the ceiling. To my right were all kinds of gifty items: paintings, plaques, pottery with Christian insignia on the sides, cards. Having never entered a store like this before, I felt as though I was being smothered with holy things. I wandered toward the back of the store, and against the back wall I saw a simple ceramic cross with a girl kneeling in prayer on it.

Perfect, I thought as I took it from its hook and headed toward the cash register. I wound my way through the aisles and found myself slowing down as I hit the book section. I love to read and even though I was so busy with the kids and my work, and the clock was ticking for me to get home, I couldn't help myself by wanting to browse just a little.

A small sign hung above one of the bookcases that said, "Catholic Books."

I walked over and began scanning the shelves for anything interesting. As I took a closer look at what the store had to offer for Catholics, all of a sudden, a few feet from me off to my left, a book suddenly fell off a shelf and landed almost directly in front of me.

I froze and could feel adrenaline rush through my body. Had anyone else seen what had happened? I quickly looked around to see if anyone had accidentally knocked it over, but no one was around me. The hair on my arms stood on end. I looked again to see if maybe someone was on the other side of the shelf. But I was alone. Slowly I moved closer to investigate.

The portrait of Mary, the mother of Jesus, on the deep-blue cover immediately caught my attention. She looked beautiful; clothed in blue and white, she was smiling gently with an expression that emanated pure love. My heart melted. I bent down and picked up the book. *Medjugorje: The Message* read the title. Next to Mary, it read: "On June 24, 1981, six children in the mountain village of Medjugorje in central Yugoslavia reported that the Virgin Mary had appeared to them on a hillside. Allegedly she has been returning every day since."

I flipped the book to the back cover and read that the book's author, Wayne Weible, was a Protestant journalist who had heard of the children's story and set about to investigate their claims.

Something about the book seemed familiar. I slowly and tenderly caressed the book cover, trying to figure out why I knew that name, Medjugorje. Then it came to me. When I was a teenager, my mother had mentioned the miracles of Medjugorje to me. She had been excited and intrigued by the prospect of what these kids had experienced. I hadn't paid much attention at that time, but now the memories of my sweet mother flooded my mind. I had been close to her—we spoke over the phone nearly every day. But she had passed away suddenly several years before. I still missed her terribly.

I started to page through the book and wondered, *Whatever happened? Had the church approved what the kids had seen?* I was sure that whatever had happened was now finished.

I put the book to my chest, determined to buy it. I thought it would be a fun and interesting read. Not every day do people see Mary, I rationalized. But also, it was a way to connect with my mom, whom I had lost nearly a decade before. Now with my book and the cross, I worked my way to the cash register. It was time to make my exit.

Halfway to the front, however, I stopped as reality came crashing back in on me.

What am I doing? I don't have time to read this. And then I thought about Drew. How would I explain that I was reading religious stuff?

I put the book on a shelf and continued toward the cash register to purchase the cross for my niece. But then another thought stopped me midway: *This is an important moment in your life. You can either leave and your life will never change, or you can go back and get that book and your life will change.*

The gauntlet had been thrown down. It was as though someone were asking me, *So what are you going to do?*

I wasn't unhappy with my life, but I wasn't completely happy with it either. That dream was still playing in my mind and making me wonder if the perfect life I thought I had was just a façade. I felt as if I stood at a crossroads. Do I step out of my comfort zone to get what I want or do I stay comfortable? I stood still for a moment. Never one to run from a challenge, I knew that if I didn't pick up that book, I would always wonder what could have been.

I went back for it. Really, what could happen from reading a simple book?

Still, as soon as I got home, I quickly and quietly went to my closet and hid the book under a pile of clothes. I may have purchased it, but I didn't need to announce that fact to my family.

That book haunted me and I had not been able to think of anything else that night since I brought it home. I had to start reading it as soon as I could. I lay in bed, next to Drew, and waited an eternity for him to drift off to sleep. Finally when I heard his breathing become deep and regular, I knew it was safe for me to retrieve the book from its secret place.

Gently I pulled back the covers and slipped quietly out of bed, tiptoeing my way to our walk-in closet. I opened the door slowly and went inside to where I had hidden the book on Medjugorje. I felt like a teenager hiding a cigarette habit from my parents!

I don't know why, but I felt uncomfortable discussing with Drew anything religious, and I especially didn't want him to know I was reading about something spiritual. I guess I was afraid I would look like a fanatic, and explaining that I was reading a book about Mary appearing on earth in our lifetime sure sounded close to being just that.

I sneaked to the family room, where I turned on the lamp next to my cozy chair. I fell into it, pulled a warm throw around me, and opened the thick paperback book.

I read the history of Medjugorje, which was a tiny parish in the distant countryside of the former Yugoslavia, today's Bosnia-Herzegovina, just over its border with Croatia. It was there, on the evening of June 25, 1981, that six children, most of them teenagers, reported to see the Blessed Virgin Mary beckoning to them from a nearby hillside. They ran to her and fell at her feet in prayer. Every day since, Mary has continued to appear to them. According to the book, her appearances were still occurring. Her messages to the children, or the visionaries, as they were known, were for the entire world: return to God, return to prayer, and live in peace with God and people.

I was deep into the book, unaware of my surroundings, when I noticed something happening to me. A numbing sensation, as though I were being shocked with electricity, was running through my entire body. As a doctor, I knew this was definitely not normal, and yet I could not think of a medical reason to explain it.

As I looked at my hands, feeling this intense sensation run through them, I suddenly received an infusion of knowledge. At that moment, I knew without any doubt, that Mary *was* real, that Jesus was real, and that God truly existed. Up until that point, I had treated God as a fairy-tale figure. I'd always wanted to believe he was real, but I'm not sure I would have bet money on it. Because I had been so scientifically and medically oriented, I was a victim of relativism: that you can believe what you want, but nobody can prove it. People told me that God existed, but I couldn't prove it. I figured God was probably real, but I wasn't totally sure. And then all of a sudden, as I read this book, I had this knowledge that without a doubt, God was real. I sat and basked in that knowledge and joy.

And then a vision flooded my mind's eye. I was alone on a large stage, standing behind a microphone and looking out at a sea of faces fixed upon me. I was speaking to them—about God and my faith in him. As quickly as the vision came, it and the feeling of electricity left my body and I found myself sitting alone in my chair with the book still in my hands.

This can't be happening, I thought. *There is no way! I mean, what in the world could I tell anyone about God? I have absolutely nothing to say about faith.*

Now deeply frightened, I flung the book across the room. I wanted it—and everything it represented—as far from me as possible. I stood and nervously began to pace. Then I began to plead with God, *No, not me, God. Please don't do this to me. I am the* last *person who should do this, and you know it!* I was shaking. *I have no story to tell!*

Then the worst thought crossed my mind: my friends and peers would know I was a Jesus freak. Me! The one who prided herself on being so practical and professional. I groaned inwardly, feeling mortified. I didn't want people to think of me as some crazy holy roller. *I'm not that person!* I told God. It just couldn't get worse than that.

But deep down in my spirit I knew that vision was true. It was going to happen—and it terrified me. I could feel bile building in my throat, making me want to throw up.

I picked up the book and tiptoed back to my bedroom closet, where I returned the book with a hardy "good riddance." Then I slipped back under the covers, next to Drew.

But sleep refused to come to me. I tossed and turned and fussed and fumed. This had been the best—and worst—night of my life. Why did I have to pick up that stupid book and read it?

CHAPTER 5

"It's My Brother's Fault"

Over the next several days my curiosity won out, and back
into the closet I went to retrieve the book and begin my secret
reading once again. The more I read, the more I wanted to know.
The book claimed that Mary asked all of her children to do several
things: to pray every day from our hearts (to really mean it), to go
to confession once a month, to fast on Wednesdays and Fridays, to
read Scripture, and always to choose peace. If we did these things,
then Mary promised that they would draw us closer to Jesus and
help us experience peace.

I was looking for peace and had been unable to find it, despite
my accomplishments and the love I held for my family. Plus I
believed Mary. Mary was a mother, and because my mother had
been so loving, I recognized Mary's love for all of us as her own
children. I was so drawn to her that I immediately loved her, not
as anything else but simply as my mother. If she said I should do

these things and they would bring me peace, I figured I might as well give them a try.

Since she gave some pretty tall orders, I decided to take them one at a time. No way was I going to fast, and the thought of going to confession terrified me. I hadn't gone since high school, and like most people I had a list of things to confess that I wasn't exactly proud of. It was too humiliating even to think about. So I decided to start with prayer.

Mary recommended that we pray the rosary every day. But the rosary is a long prayer! Following along on a strand of beads, a rosary entails saying five decades. A decade consists of one Our Father, followed by ten Hail Marys, and finally a Glory Be. That meant saying at least five Our Fathers and fifty Hail Marys!

The Our Father prayer goes:

Our Father, who art in heaven,
Hallowed be thy name.
Thy Kingdom come;
Thy will be done on earth as it is in heaven.
Give us this day our daily bread;
and forgive us our trespasses as we forgive those who trespass against us;
and lead us not into temptation, but deliver us from evil. Amen.

Then Hail Mary:

Hail Mary, full of grace.
The Lord is with thee.
Blessed art thou amongst women,

And blessed is the fruit of thy womb,
Jesus.
Holy Mary, Mother of God,
Pray for us sinners,
Now and at the hour of our death.
Amen.

And then finally, the rosary ends with the Glory Be:

Glory be to the Father, Son, and the Holy Spirit.
As it was in the beginning is now and ever shall be.
World without end. Amen.

Praying was the most difficult thing I had ever done. Because the rosary is so repetitive, before I knew it, I would get distracted, thinking about dinner that night or when to pick up the kids, and then I realized I had stop praying. Plus I didn't even own a rosary! I had to use my fingers to try to keep count.

Determined, I would start over, but soon my mind would again wander. Frustrated with my failure, finally I decided to pray only one decade. That seemed like something I could do. After weeks of this, I added on another decade, then another, until finally I could pray the entire rosary.

But I was still keeping my new spiritual awakening a secret from my family. I continually prayed on my knees in my bedroom closet with the door shut, always listening for someone who might approach. I did not want Drew to find me. That would bring up a conversation I didn't want to have. I would have to tell him I truly believed in God, and that Christ had become an important part of my life. I would have to reveal what had happened to me.

Even through that fear, I found myself changing. I had an overwhelming desire to please God in any way that I could. So I started to attend mass three times a week and pray the rosary every day. But to make matters worse (in my mind), I had an irrepressible drive to go to Medjugorje and see this place where miracles occurred. I needed to see it and learn everything I could about that place. While I was so excited by the thought of going, I had a big problem: at least I could pray in my closet. How could I possibly travel halfway around the world and not tell Drew why or where I was going?

What could I possibly say to him that wouldn't make me sound like a lunatic?

Hey, honey, guess what? I've had this supernatural conversion happen to me and I really believe in Jesus. Oh, and by the way, I want to go to this remote village on the other side of the world where the Mother of God keeps appearing.

I groaned just at the thought of how that news would go over.

I prayed, desperately seeking a way to bring it up so that he would accept it and I wouldn't sound like a nut.

Finally, the inner drive wouldn't let go of me—I knew I had to go to Medjugorje, but I also knew I couldn't confess that to Drew—so I gave the problem to Mary.

"I am too weak, Mary. I'm sorry. I know I'm failing you here. I know you want me to go, and I don't have the courage to ask my husband and I don't think I ever will. So if you want me to go, you're going to have it make it happen."

A few weeks after my Medjugorje prayer to Mary, I traveled alone to St. Louis to see my brothers Mike and Tom—something

I tried to do at least once a year. One evening, my younger brother, Tom, and I were together in his kitchen, laughing and talking about old memories, when I mentioned that I had to get something from my room to show him. Tom followed me, and as he waited while I found what I needed, he noticed the Medjugorje book on my bedside table.

"What's that?" he asked.

I froze as I tried to figure out what to say. *Should I tell him the truth?* I wondered. I looked at Tom and he seemed genuinely interested. "It's a book about Mary appearing to some teenagers."

As I began to explain the basics of the story to him, his eyes lit up.

"Mom talked about Medjugorje," he said.

"Yeah, she mentioned it to me too." I could see that this might be his connection to Mom, just as it had originally been for me.

"Could I... read it? I mean, when you're done with it?"

Immediately I picked up the book and handed it to him.

He cradled it in his hands as if I had given him a treasure. "Thanks," he said and smiled brightly. He noticed the bookmark toward the last pages, so he handed it back. "Go ahead and finish it while you're here, then I'll read it."

When I returned home, sans the book (which was actually a relief, because I wouldn't have to struggle with hiding it!), I continued with my daily routine of working and praying and keeping my secret from the rest of my family. Within a few days of being home, while I was pushing my sons on some swings at a nearby park, my cell phone rang.

"I finished the book," Tom said. "So has Anne." It had only been three days! That thick book had taken me two weeks to read, and Tom and his wife *both* read it in *three days*? "Listen, I can't explain this but we really want to go. And we want you to come too."

"To Medjugorje?" I forgot about pushing the boys. Goosebumps covered my arms. All I could think was, *Mary, you work fast.*

"Yes! I just want to go there. I want to check everything out. I want to see it!"

I couldn't believe that my brother shared my unexplainable enthusiasm for going to see this place. "I know, I know!" I told him, laughing.

After I hung up the phone, I felt like I was in a daze. I'd just agreed to go to this holy site—and I hadn't even told my husband! Now it was real. I had to spill my secret. I would be gone for a week, maybe more. That meant Drew would have to take care of the boys by himself.

Then I had another paralyzing realization: my peers would find out. I couldn't just drop my work schedule.

Somehow I'd naively thought that I could just go experience it and then come back without anyone finding out. I *was* crazy.

For days I searched for ways to broach the subject, but it never seemed the right time or opportunity. A week passed, and even though I hadn't told Drew, I'd wasted no time on the internet investigating Medjugorje tours. But still my silence on the subject was deafening.

Another week passed and I finally sensed I had the right opportunity. Drew was going to San Francisco for a medical conference and had invited me to go with him—sort of for a mini-vacation. This was perfect. I would tell him there.

The trip was relaxing and romantic—except I held this nagging anxiety that I would have to tell Drew. While he was in meetings during the day, I would walk around the city and think, *What am I going to do? I have to ask him.* But even in San Francisco, no place or time seemed just right. Until the final night of our trip.

We sat at a lovely, intimate Italian restaurant, making small talk and eating our house salads, when it came to me: *I can blame my brother!*

It was a brilliant idea. I couldn't believe I hadn't thought of it before!

I poured us both a large glass of wine from the bottle we were enjoying, and then looked seriously at Drew. "I'm a little worried about something."

"Really? What's up?" My face must have registered my concern, because he put his fork down and looked directly into my eyes.

My pulse began to beat a little faster, so I took a sip of wine. "It's about Tom," I said, hoping my voice stayed steady. "Well, you know... I guess there's this place called Medjugorje. It's in Bosnia-Herzegovina. And Tom read this book about it. I guess Mary our Mother is appearing over there to six kids. At least that's what this book says. And he wants to go check it out. I think he's kind of lost his mind."

"What?"

"Yeah, I know. It's completely crazy. And what's worse is that he invited me to go with him."

Drew's eyes got big. "Are you serious? Well, do you *want* to go?"

It was now or never, so I dove in deeper. "Drew, honestly, I think I have to go. This really isn't like Tom. I think he might be going a little off the deep end. I just want to keep an eye on him. You know how people get taken advantage of and I don't want him to fall victim, I want to make sure he's okay." My lies and fears were making me a wreck inside. I hated being less than honest with

Drew—we'd always told each other the truth—but I was so afraid of what he would think of me.

"Well, if you think you should go, then go, but I really don't want to go with you guys. Is that okay with you? I mean, if you really want me to go, I will, but I would much rather stay at home with the boys."

I could see by the look in his eyes, he was sincere. He had nothing against me going, he was just terrified that I was asking him to join us! Relief washed over me as I reached again for my glass. "No, I'm not asking you to go at all," I reassured him. "I don't think both of us need to go. I just really think I need to watch out for Tom."

Now I watched relief flush over him!

Within hours of our return home, I called Tom to tell him I would definitely join them on their trip and that I couldn't wait. Even though I'd already done some preliminary research on tour groups, I kept seeing them listed as "pilgrimages," which made me nervous. I wasn't quite sure what that meant, but I didn't want to be stuck with a group of genuine nuts!

Fortunately, Tom had been doing some research as well. He'd recently gone to a party where he had met a young man who had returned from Medjugorje only a few weeks earlier. He had recommended we go with Pilgrim's Peace Center, run out of Florida by Sandy and Mike Tobin. This man had loved his trip and spoke highly of Sandy and Mike.

I looked them up and was impressed. They seemed personable and fun, and not only would they make sure we experienced everything in Medjugorje, they guaranteed that we would actually stay with Vicka, one of the six original teenagers, or visionaries, in her home.

I couldn't believe we could actually see one of the visionaries and stay in her home! I called that day and made reservations for the three of us to accompany Sandy and Mike on their next trip, which was six months away in May 2001.

So everything was set. We made our deposits, reserved our flights, and began to count the days until we left.

CHAPTER 6
Signs and Wonders

N ow that the trip to Medjugorje was a reality, I knew I should begin to prepare spiritually for whatever I might encounter there. So I became more intentional about doing all the things Mary had encouraged believers to do, which I'd read about in the Medjugorje book. I prayed the rosary every day and I attended mass more than once a week. (I still hadn't gone to confession, but I figured I'd inch my way up to that.)

I worked in my office two and a half days a week, so on the days I wasn't at my medical practice, I dropped off the kids at school and then headed over to attend the eight o'clock mass.

But still I did everything in secret. No one knew that I was becoming more sincere and serious about my faith. Which made my next step incredibly difficult.

For months the boys had come home with brochures inviting parents to go to a rosary prayer group. With each notice I'd think,

Oh, that's nice. But I wasn't going to get involved with that. It was too public for me.

One morning as I dropped off my son Johnny at his preschool, I heard that one of the fathers had passed away suddenly that morning. Although he had been diagnosed with leukemia only a few months earlier, his quick passing had been unexpected.

The news ripped at my heart. How was this family going to survive? How could his wife raise their five small children all by herself? What must those children be feeling?

I wanted to do something for this family, to support them any way I could. Immediately I went to the office and offered to pay tuition for their child who was in my son's class. I needed to do more though. But what?

From deep inside me I felt an intense call to pray. At that moment I remembered the rosary prayer group. I could do that. And others had to join me in praying. I no longer cared that someone might find out about my faith—this wasn't about me. A family needed our prayers, and we had to send up as many prayers as possible.

I quickly dropped off my son Drew at his classroom at his school and headed to the church where the rosary group met. I walked into the room and immediately found a seat as far from the action as I could get. I looked around. About twenty-five women were there. Everyone seemed to know each other and were happily talking amongst themselves. I vaguely knew Martha, the woman who had started the gathering. She had always been kind and encouraging to me.

Now as I settled into my seat, I began to second guess my decision. *What if they're all whackos? I don't want to be linked with fanatics*, I thought as I spied the exit and tried to figure how to leave without anyone noticing.

Unfortunately, everyone noticed me enter and sit. As each pair of eyes landed on me, I thought, *Oh great, I'm the newbie too. More attention.*

But then one person after another approached and warmly greeted me. They all seemed,,, normal. Kind, even. They made me feel comfortable.

When the meeting began Martha asked if anyone had any special intentions. I spoke up, and with great effort not to cry, explained what had happened. The women seemed as devastated as I was. As we prayed the rosary together, I felt such comfort and peace. I knew I had done something substantial for a family in need. And the prayer group wasn't some awful group of crazies. In fact I liked these women very much.

Life was good. I was consistently praying and was now a full-fledged member of the school's rosary prayer group—even if my husband still didn't have a clue. One step at a time, I figured. I felt stronger in my faith. Everything seemed to be falling into place and the void I'd felt for so long slowly started to fill with love and peace.

My career was going well. My family was happy. I felt fairly complete.

At 10 a.m. one morning I was scheduled to operate on a women's face to remove a basal cell carcinoma, a common form of skin cancer. As I was suturing up her cheek, I heard this distinct voice say, *You need to tell Jesus that you love him.*

The voice was so clear in my head that I stopped mid-stitch.

That's wild, I thought, as I realized that I had no idea where that voice would have come from. It certainly wouldn't have originated with me.

Huh-hum. A nurse next to me cleared her throat and moved slightly, which jarred me back to my task.

I started working the needle again, but couldn't shake the thought, *I need to tell Jesus that I love him.* But why?

God is an all-knowing, all-powerful God. He knew I loved him; I didn't have to say it. I shook off the thought.

Three days later, I was with my sons Johnny and Jack. We were holding hands as we walked and chatted together. All of a sudden the voice returned, *You need to tell Jesus that you love him.*

That's that same wild thought, I told myself. I was enthralled, but not enough to follow the suggestion. Instead, again, I simply dismissed it.

Every day the thought returned. I would be at the gym working out or fixing dinner or running errands and it would come to me. Always subtle and gentle, but always clear.

With each occurrence, I followed it with, *This is weird. This is a recurrent thought that I'm not creating.*

After several weeks, I became angry at it. Since one of my many flaws is that I don't like to be told what to do, I naturally rebelled and began to argue with the thought when it would come.

No, I don't need to do that. Why does Jesus need to hear that I love him? He already knows how I feel. I pray every day. I attend mass. Isn't that what's important? God knows. He should know that I love him because I'm doing these things for him. I mean, how else would I show that I love him? He's got to know that I love him! Why do I have to say it?

No matter the brilliant arguments I made for my case, the same thought continued every day.

Six weeks passed. Not only was I frustrated, but now I was simply weary. I was tired of fighting the voice, fatigued with trying to come up with any new excuse not to obey. I don't know why I so stubbornly resisted, but I just couldn't bring myself to say those three simple words to my Savior: *I. Love. You.*

One night I was jolted awake.

You need to tell Jesus that you love him.

That the voice could awaken me from a deep sleep scared me. I realized the thought had to be from God. It *was* real.

So in the darkness, I nodded my agreement. I would tell him. But I needed to do it properly: in a church—a holy place—kneeling at the altar. With my agreement, I fell back to sleep.

Only, the next time I was in church, I didn't follow through.

A week went by and I had forgotten about my promise. The thought no longer plagued me, so I didn't feel the need to pursue the matter. I drove to the gym, as I did every morning for my daily exercise routine. As I stepped onto the elliptical machine, I glanced down and noticed that my left shoelace had come untied.

I knelt to tie my laces and was overcome by the most forceful and urgent voice in my head: *YOU NEED TO TELL JESUS YOU LOVE HIM.*

It wasn't mean, but the tone was strong, as if God were telling me to quit messing around.

I had to tell him right then. I knew if I didn't, my pride would get in the way.

Okay, fine. I'll do it, I thought. I felt a little like a teenager whose mom keeps badgering her to clean her room and she finally agrees—just to get her mom off her back.

You know, God, I continued, *I wanted to do this in a holy place. I'm in the middle of the gym in Southern California. But since I'm already down on one knee, I'm just going to go for it. It's the best I got right now, because if I don't do it now, it's not going to happen.*

I sighed inwardly, took a deep breath, and then whispered, "Jesus, I love you with my entire heart. I love you with everything that I have."

All of a sudden I found myself—still on my knees, holding my laces—pouring out my heart. "I no longer want my will to be done in my life. I want only your will to be done. And use me to bring other people to you."

As I spoke the words, this amazing feeling of peace washed over me. Part of it must have been relief that it was finally done. But it was also this wonderful feeling that I'd actually said the words.

And nothing crazy happened. No one stopped working out to point and laugh. No earthquakes. No TV news cameras. Just a feeling of completeness. I'd thought that praying daily and attending mass felt good—it was nothing compared to how I felt at that moment! I truly felt whole for the first time in my life.

As I stepped onto the elliptical machine, I began mentally kicking myself. *Why did you make that so hard? Look how good you feel now. It wasn't difficult. And it's over, and there was no big deal—and you made it such a big deal.*

I laughed aloud and then whispered again: "I love you, Jesus."

I realized that Jesus wasn't commanding me to tell him I loved him, as I had believed and fought against. He was simply opening my heart to his peace and love. He was showing me he wanted a deeper relationship with me, not as an authoritarian figure but as a true friend, someone who knew me and deeply loved me.

That is what he desires from all his children. Just as we constantly need to hear we are loved, so does our God. He is no different. After all, we are made in his image. My prayers up to that point had been to a God who was somehow removed, distant, and aloof. I had never thought of Jesus as being so "personal." Now they became more intimate. Now I wasn't just talking to the God of the universe, I was talking to a close, intimate friend.

Three days later, early in the morning, I was driving in the back canyons of San Diego County, enjoying the rugged landscape. Small scraggly rounds of scrub brush were scattered over the hills of rocky, sandy soil, which lined the roadways. It was a warm, sunny day with only a few wisps of clouds scattered over the sky. My three boys—ages six, four, and two—were buckled up in the back of our minivan. We were headed to San Diego's Wild Animal Park. The boys loved riding the tram amid the herds of animals living in their natural habitats. So as I drove we laughed and talked about all the animals we were going to see.

"The gorillas!" one of the boys cried out, while the other two chimed in with yeses and cheers. The gorilla exhibit was their favorite, and so we always saved that one for last. The boys couldn't wait.

I came to a T-shaped intersection, one of the last turns I had to make before coming to the park's entrance, about a mile and a half away. I stopped and checked to my left for any oncoming traffic. The road was empty. I made the right-hand turn, glanced into the sky directly in front of me, and froze. The car sat idly as I forced myself to blink hard several times.

That... isn't... possible.

But the more I stared at the sky, the more I knew I couldn't deny what was there. I was looking... at Jesus.

His face filled the huge, open sky. Made up of layers of hundreds of white clouds, I could see every detail of his face: his eyelashes, the pupils of his eyes, his long even nose, his well-kept, short beard, and his shoulder length, slightly wavy, thick hair. I could see the crow's feet extending from his eyes, and his perfect, even teeth as he smiled broadly at me. I could actually sense joy coming from him.

I couldn't believe this was actually happening. It defied all the laws of nature. And why was he showing himself to me?

I couldn't talk, much less move. I sat in awe and wonder; I was actually looking at the face of God!

Oh my God, you are real. You are so real, I thought as goose bumps covered my arms and the back of my neck.

The only person I knew who had seen Jesus in the sky was Saint Paul, and his life changed dramatically because of it. Dread broke into the joy and thrill I felt. This was obviously a sign. So what did this mean for me?

Something is going to happen in my life, I realized. Somehow I sensed that whatever it was, it wasn't going to be good. So while I was grateful that I saw the formation, I also wished I hadn't.

I don't know what you're asking of me, God. I think you're going to ask something of me, and I hope I'm strong enough to live through it.

I never asked my boys to look. I never even reached for the camera, which sat on the front seat next to me. And I knew I wouldn't tell Drew—or anybody else—about it. Somehow I knew this was for me alone. Plus who would believe me? I was a physician. And doctors don't have those kinds of experiences. Even so, I knew it was real. And I knew it meant something.

After several minutes, the clouds began to break up and slowly drift away. And then he was gone.

I thought I'd placed my foot on the brake, but I had unknowingly let the car creep along the road. Once I broke the trance, I saw that the car had slowly moved toward the road's shoulder. I glanced quickly in the rearview mirror to see if I was holding up any traffic. Fortunately, no other cars were around me. The boys were giggling about something, completely unaware of what I had just experienced.

I was stunned. That day I had a difficult time remaining present with the boys. As they laughed and rejoiced in seeing all the animals, I couldn't stop thinking about what I had witnessed and what it possibly meant for me.

Two weeks later, I discovered I was pregnant.

CHAPTER 7
The Admission

Drew and I were over the moon with the news that I was pregnant. After our third son, Jack, was born, I'd wanted to get pregnant again right away. I know that sounds crazy—especially since I'd originally not wanted to have any kids! And then I "gave in" and figured Drew and I would be content with a typical family of four—us, along with two children. When Drew wanted to go for a third child, I had been resistant to the idea. But after we had Jack, he became my life-changing baby. That's when I realized I really *wanted* to be a mom. All those years of my determination to have a career and remain single seemed so far away now. Motherhood had become my life. So I was ready to jump right in and have a fourth one!

But for some reason I couldn't get pregnant. With my other kids, it seemed as if I'd get pregnant, *snap*, no problem. With this fourth baby, though, Drew and I tried for three years. And then all of a sudden, I was pregnant.

Drew had always wanted a daughter—and this became a real possibility for us. To be fair, he didn't want just one daughter. He would have twenty children if he could!

I was thrilled because after three years of infertility, I thought our family was done. Plus I was getting older. I was now almost forty—nearing geriatric in the medical fertility world.

So I knew this baby was special. Our fourth child was meant to be.

An added excitement was that I realized I would be carrying my baby while I was in Medjugorje. I wanted this one to receive a special blessing. I would be three months pregnant while I was there, so maybe the child was part of the reason I was supposed to go on this journey.

Although I talked freely about the baby, I rarely mentioned my upcoming trip, which I was just as thrilled about. But when I had to let people know I was going to be out of town, I would simply say I was going to Croatia on a medical mission trip. Even though I really could have done some medical work there, I just wanted to go and soak in the sanctity of the place.

Not too long before I left for the trip, I attended a going-away party for a former colleague from the clinic where I did my fellowship.

One of my friends from the clinic told me, "I think that's so cool you're going on this trip."

"I know, I can't wait. I think it's going to be great."

"I've always wanted to do something like that," she said.

As we talked, a heavy feeling settled in my chest. I pushed it aside and continued to mingle. But later, after I said my goodbyes and walked out, the feeling returned. It was as if Mary were whispering, *You sadden me when you don't tell the truth. Why do you refuse to acknowledge me? Do I embarrass you?*

I couldn't believe it. I was so afraid of what people would think that I was willing to lie about the Mother of God. And so I turned around, went back inside, and walked straight over to my friend.

I inhaled deeply and went for it. "Katie, I'm going on that trip to do a little bit of medical work, but the main reason I'm going is because Mary, the Mother of God, is appearing over there and I want to check it out."

Her eyes grew to the size of plates.

I swallowed hard. "I've got to go. I'll see you later." Then I turned before she could say anything and walked back out. I could feel her eyes follow me as I left. I was shaking, but I was also proud. I had stood up for my faith and for Mary, whom I had loved deeply.

To this day I have no idea what my friend thinks of that whole thing, but I did it. And that made a big change in my life. Because I was either going to own up to the fact that my faith was important and I *was* changing or I was just going to hide my whole life.

I was taking baby steps. But I realized that baby steps are still steps.

PART 2

Medjugorje

CHAPTER 8

The First Night

Finally, after waiting six months, in May 2001, I was leaving for Medjugorje! For the next eleven days I was set to see and experience things I couldn't even imagine. I flew from San Diego to Seattle and met up with a few other "pilgrims," as the tour company called us, including Jim, one of the leaders. From Seattle we flew to Atlanta, and then to Amsterdam and connected with the others, forty-two in all. That's where I met up with my brother Tom and sister-in-law Anne.

I felt odd being called a pilgrim, though in one sense, I suppose that's what we were. The tour leaders had sent us large nametags to help us identify one another in the airports. But I thought that was goofy. I hadn't even told my closest friends and coworkers about the real purpose of the trip, so why would I want to announce it to the entire flying community? My nametag stayed in my bag.

It was during the layover in Amsterdam that several members of our group passed out prayer books and songbooks. They announced we were going to sing and praise the Lord.

You have got to be kidding me. I was thrown out of the high school choir because I couldn't carry a tune. So that's the last thing I wanted to do. And then to be a spectacle in the airport singing a holy song? I couldn't think of anything worse.

"Okay, I'm going to go to the bathroom," I told the group. "I'll be right back."

"I'm going to go with her," Tom said quickly.

"Wait for me," Anne said.

"Who are those people?" I asked, as soon as I was sure we were out of earshot. Just then the group began to sing loudly, proclaiming their faith. We quickly picked up our step. I couldn't get away fast enough!

For a moment I began to wonder what we'd gotten ourselves into. But we'd committed to the trip—with this specific group of people—so we decided just to laugh it off and make the best of it.

The trip was arduous and exhausting. From Amsterdam we flew to Zagreb, Croatia, and then to Split, Croatia. From there, we hopped on a bus for a three-and-a-half-hour ride to Medjugorje, in Bosnia-Herzegovina. It was around 7:30 p.m. when we got on the bus, so there was still enough daylight to see. I halfway wished it had been dark out, though. The drive was terrifying as the bus careened back and forth as it climbed its way up the side of a steep and dangerous cliff. The road consisted of nothing but two narrow lanes and sharp ninety-degree switchbacks. To make matters worse, there was not a guardrail in sight. Seeing the Adriatic Sea below us was spectacular, but my mind couldn't take in the full beauty because it was more concerned about the way the bus leaned toward the edge with every curve.

The trip took more than twenty-four hours from start to finish. And by the time we arrived at 11 p.m. their time, I was dead tired.

The bus pulled in front of the family home of Vicka, one of the original teens who had seen Mary in 1981. We were staying here. Vicka and her family lived in a small portion of the home while the rest had been built to house pilgrims.

And at some point during our stay, Vicka would talk to our group alone, and if we were fortunate, we might even be able to witness one of her daily apparitions with Mary.

We unloaded our bags and everyone headed off to their assigned rooms to get some much-needed rest. We would start the official tour the next morning. Even though I was exhausted, I wasn't ready to go to my room yet. We were in Medjugorje! I didn't want to just head off to bed. Tom admitted the same thing, so he and I stayed outside, while Anne went to their room. We tried to make out our surroundings, but the night was pitch black and extremely quiet, except for an occasional call from a rooster somewhere off in the distance.

As we stood, gazing up at the numerous brilliant stars, we heard the approaching crunch of footsteps on the gravel. One of our group broke through the darkness. A man of average height, thin with an athletic build, and appearing to be in his late fifties, I recognized him as Jim, one of the leaders I'd met in Seattle.

He had been to Medjugorje several times before and was heading to the top of Apparition Hill where Mary first appeared. Since we were still up, he asked if we wanted to join him.

Are you kidding? I thought, and said excitedly, "Yes!"

He told us he'd wait while we grabbed our flashlights from our luggage, which someone had already taken to our rooms. We were heading on our first Medjugorje adventure.

We slowly made our way through the dark night with the beams of our flashlights falling upon the village's small stone houses and souvenir shops. The gravel road turned to a cobblestone path, which was lined with gifts shops on either side. It was amazing to think that this tiny village had hosted more than thirty million visitors.

Although Medjugorje is now located in Bosnia-Herzegovina, when the apparitions first began, it was part of Communist-controlled Yugoslavia. The story goes that on the evening of June 24, 1981, two teenage girls, Mirjana and Ivanka, were out walking. At one point during their walk, Ivanka looked up and noticed the figure of a woman on one of the hillsides. She immediately recognized her as the Blessed Mother and wanted Mirjana to look. Mirjana thought Ivanka was joking and replied simply, "Why would Our Lady appear to us?" and refused even to look.

Before long, they saw other teenagers from the village—Vicka, Ivan, and Milka—and Ivanka told them what she had seen. Curious, they all followed Ivanka to the place she had witnessed Mary. When they arrived, they saw the figure, bathed in light and wearing a shimmering silver-gray gown. She held the baby Jesus and motioned for them to come to her, but they all ran away in fear. Vicka fled so fast that she literally ran out of her shoes.

The children told their families what they had seen, but most of their families did not believe them. Vicka's mother, however, told her to take holy water with her, and if she ever saw the vision again, she was to sprinkle it on the figure and command the devil to leave. If the vision were truly from God, it would stay.

The next day, at about the same time they had seen the figure the night before, the teenagers felt an intense desire to return to the hill. Milka's mother had taken her to work in a distant family field. When the soon-to-be-visionaries came by to get Milka and found her absent, her sister Marija was asked to join them, as well as Marija's cousin, ten-year old Jakov, who also happened to be at the house.

The six children approached the area and suddenly saw a bright flash. Looking again, they saw the shimmering figure on the hill, motioning to them to draw near. The children ran up the rocky slope, fell on their knees in front of her.

She identified herself as the Blessed Virgin Mary. When the children asked her why she had come, she answered, "I have come to tell you that God exists and he loves you. Let the others who do not see me believe as you do."

The next evening, the children again felt an inner urge within them to return. This time Vicka sprinkled holy water on the figure, made the sign of the cross, and commanded the vision to leave if it was not from God. At that, the figure simply smiled and spoke to them with great tenderness and warmth.

The news of the apparition spread quickly and soon thousands of people flocked to Medjugorje—in particular to Apparition Hill.

Now I was joining the thousands—millions—of pilgrims who came to see, to pray, and to experience the miracles that occurred at this special place Mary had chosen to reach out to humanity. As we reached the base of Apparition Hill, or *Podboro*, as it is known in Croatian, I noticed a stark difference in the landscape. The path was no longer paved with cobblestone. Instead large jagged rocks and loose scattered stones were spread everywhere.

While only moderately steep, the hill became treacherous in the obscurity of the night. Slowly we wound our way up the path, at times waiting and shining our lights down on the rocks so we could see our way. After what seemed to be about twenty minutes of climbing, we arrived at the original spot where Mary first appeared. A tall aluminum metal cross marked the spot. (Today a large marble statue of Our Lady stands there.) Finding some larger rocks to sit on, we noticed other people near us, silent in prayer. One by one they made their way down the hill, and Tom, Jim, and I found ourselves alone.

We began to share stories of our faith and why each of us had come to Medjugorje. Tom spoke first. He shared how excited he was to be there. That he'd read the book about this place and he really wanted to see what would happen here. I spoke next, but all I could say was that I simply wanted to see the people here and how they loved their faith. But deep down I wanted so much more. I wanted to experience everything I could. I wanted to see miracles. I wanted to touch God.

After a few moments, Jim reached into his pants pocket and pulled out a vial of oil. "Why don't we start praying?"

He placed a dab of oil in the sign of the cross on Tom's forehead and said a quiet prayer over him. Then he moved to me and repeated the action. As soon as his hand touched my forehead, I felt as though my body were going to start to float. It became very light and I started to fall backward. But I caught myself and straightened up.

After he'd finished, I told him, "You know when you blessed me, I felt like I was going to pass out." He just smiled and walked on.

Then we spent some quiet time in prayer. I prayed to know God more and for my family to be safe and experience what I was learning in my faith. Finally, Jim stood to leave. Instead of returning down the hill the way we'd come, he took us on a steeper, more rugged and direct route. At the bottom, we found ourselves near a small, secluded area with stone benches in front of a large wooden cross painted blue. A small statue of Mary stood in front of the cross.

"This is the Blue Grotto," Jim told us. I knew it was also called the Blue Cross, named for the six-foot-tall cross painted blue.

"What's the significance?" I asked.

Jim shrugged. "None really. Ivan, the visionary who painted the cross, used blue. But Ivan's prayer group meets here. Mary asked him to start a group specifically to pray for the youth of the world."

Suddenly, I was overwhelmed by the scent of roses. It was so strong that I thought I must be standing in the middle of thousands of roses.

Wow, this must be really beautiful in the daylight. I can't wait to see it! I scanned the area with my flashlight expecting to see a beautiful garden. At the foot of the cross were a small bunch of flowers. As I stepped closer to them, I saw they were plastic. There were no flowers, no plants of any kind. No bushes. Not even grass. Only rocks. I couldn't understand where this powerful scent was coming from.

We found a little stone bench and sat. I nestled between Tom and Jim and again we began to pray. In my heart I thanked Mary for calling me to this place. I was enjoying the peace and solitude, when I noticed Jim slide off the bench and crumble to his knees. It looked as if someone had pushed him. I thought he might be having heart attack. Just as I started to ask him if he was all right, I heard him say, "My children, thank you so much for coming. You have made my Son very happy."

Could this be Mary? I wondered. *What is going on?*

"Place your hands over your heart."

Not really understanding what was happening, and yet still believing that this was Mary speaking, I placed my hands over my heart. I saw Tom do the same.

"Take your heart out of your chest and offer it up to my Son, Jesus."

I did so, imagining my heart within my hands as I lifted them toward the night sky.

All was silent for a moment. Then Jim spoke again. "You may place your hearts back in your chests now. You have made my Son so very happy. Enjoy nature, enjoy your lives; they are as fleeting as that of a flower."

Slowly and with some difficulty, Jim rose and sat back on the bench next to me. He looked wiped out, as if he'd just used up all his energy.

I remained silent, with my hands still at my chest. It seemed as if Mary had spoken through him. But how? Finally, my curiosity got the best of me and I had to know.

"Jim," I whispered. "Was that Mary?"

"Uh huh," he replied uncomfortably.

"So how do you... do that?"

"I don't know." He paused. "It began happening several years ago on a trip here. I discussed it with several priests from my home diocese as well as from this area. I'd hoped they would offer guidance and direction. We prayed for discernment. I went through so much evaluation including what I thought at the time were two exorcisms, but they were really intense prayer sessions to determine the nature of what was going on. But finally, everyone felt it seemed to be some private revelation from Mary. We've all agreed that I need to watch it closely, and I have a spiritual director who helps me—especially since obviously private revelation is not considered part of the Divine Faith."

I had never heard of such a thing. I knew Mary had appeared to people over the years. There were well known church-approved shrines in Fatima, Portugal, and Lourdes, France, to celebrate such occurrences in the past. And I knew those were also considered to be private revelation and not something the church required Catholics to accept or believe. But I had never heard of Mary *speaking* through people.

As we made our way back to Vicka's home, I kept trying to wrap my head around everything I'd just experienced, when suddenly it hit me. The roses!

"Jim, I smelled roses at the Blue Grotto, but I didn't see any flowers anywhere."

Jim smiled. "That's Mary. When she appears, she often comes in the scent of roses."

I almost tripped over my steps. I had been in the presence of Mary—*my baby* had been in the presence of Mary! I couldn't believe this treasure that I'd just received. God was smiling on me for sure. I'd been in this holy place less than two hours and had already encountered my first miracle. I couldn't wait to see what else this trip would bring.

CHAPTER 9

Making a Deal with God

I tossed and turned all that night. I was exhausted from the travel, but I couldn't sleep. I was struggling to understand everything that had happened the previous night and what it all could mean. And if that were not enough, there was the constant nagging reality that God wanted me to speak publicly about my faith. I groaned inwardly every time I thought about it.

My brain simply wouldn't turn off to allow me to rest.

Finally, at dawn, I slipped out of the house before anyone awoke and retraced my steps to Apparition Hill. I was the only one out that early. The climb was much easier in early morning light, but still I had to watch my footing on the jagged rocks. Many of the stones were loose, and many others were worn smooth from years of use. Combined with the light morning dew, they were extremely slippery.

At the top, I stood before the large metal cross and said a brief prayer and then I moved to a nearby rock to sit. I took out my rosary, and as I prayed, the vision of my speaking in front of thousands of people returned. It was so vivid, as though if I opened my eyes, I would see the microphone in front of me. My heart felt as if it weighed a thousand pounds. That vision haunted me, and I just couldn't handle what I knew God was asking me to do. I didn't *want* to be that person. I didn't want to be the crazy lady who always talked about Jesus. No way.

"God, I know you exist and I know you're asking me to speak about my faith..." I began to pray the rosary with intensity. Five mysteries or decades.

I prayed a second rosary. But still I felt such a burden. Then I prayed a third entire rosary. Fifteen mysteries, fifteen decades. I had never prayed more than one set of mysteries in my life.

Tears filled my eyes as I listed the many reasons why I was not the person for the job. I felt a little like Moses at the burning bush, who kept explaining to God why he wasn't the right choice to lead the Israelites out of Egypt and into the Promised Land. I was too weak, too afraid, not a great public speaker, and I didn't have a single thing to talk about. No one would listen to me anyway. I didn't have a story to tell.

I didn't *want* to say no to God, but I couldn't see another way. The thought that I was going to fail my God was heart wrenching.

In my desperation, I opened my eyes and scanned the horizon. On an adjacent mountain, I saw a large white cross sitting at the top. I remembered from my reading about this place that this was Mount Krizevac, also known as Cross Mountain. The mountain itself was almost a mile high, with a much steeper rocky path than the one I was on. Along its path were the fourteen Stations of the

Cross. Stations of the Cross are a favorite devotion of Catholics in which they remember in prayer every important aspect of Christ's Passion and death. The path ends at the top of the mountain at the base of a large, white concrete cross that contains a relic, or special blessed piece, of the actual true cross Jesus was crucified on. The local villagers had built the cross in 1933 to commemorate the 1900th anniversary of Christ's crucifixion.

As I gazed at the cross, I opened my heart to God and intensely prayed.

God, I know you are asking me to speak to others about my faith, but I can't. I'm the wrong person for you. I know I'm failing you. But I can do three things for you. With your help, I can live a life so that my husband will believe in you as much as I do. I can raise our children in a true Christian home and environment so they will have faith in you as well. And...

I took a deep breath and then continued.

And I can bring one more soul to you. These are the things I can do, Lord. Please, if that is enough for you, let me know.

Just then an idea popped into my mind. The cross! I had read stories about the cross on Mount Krizevac. Some people have reported that they've seen it spinning on its vertical axis, others have seen the cross ablaze with fire, while still others have seen the cross completely disappear from view.

I closed my eyes and prayed: *God, if those three things are enough for you, and I don't have to speak, please make that cross over there disappear. If you do that, then I will know.*

I knew it was crazy to try to bargain with God, but I was so desperate to get out of what I knew he was asking of me. With tremendous hope and anticipation, I opened my eyes.

The cross was gone.

I blinked hard and looked again. Nothing. The sky was clear so it wasn't as though the cross was hiding behind fog or a cloud. *It's probably the refraction of the sun hitting it in a certain way,* I thought. *It's still there, I just don't see it at this angle.* I got off the rock and walked to my right several yards. No cross.

I'm still at that same angle, I realized. *I'll just go down the hill a little bit.* So I walked down the hill, but even there I didn't see it.

My jaw dropped as I kept straining to look, to see something, anything on Mount Krizevac.

It was gone.

A flood of relief washed over me as I realized I did not have to speak!

"Thank you, God!" I said aloud in almost a sigh. The one prayer I'd needed answered had been. *Thank you, thank you, God!*

I was full of energy as I ran down Apparition Hill. The heavy weight had been lifted off of me and I was happy! I didn't care what happened the rest of the trip. I felt as though I'd taken the last exam of my entire life. I was free!

CHAPTER 10
More Signs

For the next week I opened myself to experiencing as much as I could from this place that had already proven to be miraculous. Every morning at dawn, I'd sneak out of my simple, yellow-painted, cinderblock-walled room and head back up to Apparition Hill to meditate and pray. I no longer carried the heavy burden of God asking me to speak publicly about my faith, so I was able to concentrate on other issues. I prayed for my family, for our future, and of course for the life I carried in my womb. I felt such a special connection to Mary as I prayed in this place since I was pregnant. I knew she understood my worries and concerns about motherhood. My silent, private time there felt filled with grace, and with each day that passed I began to notice something unmistakable. Deep within my heart, I felt this overflowing sense of peace and joy. I realized that all those years of my searching for meaning, for something more in my life, had brought me to this place. Who knew that peace would come from God?

After I returned from the hill, I'd join the rest of our group for a breakfast of eggs or French toast and then we'd hike a mile down a worn, red-dirt path through small, well-tended vineyards and into the village bulging with tourist souvenir shops and cafes to Saint James Church, the community's local parish, to attend the ten o'clock English mass.

The church's two large bell towers rose high above the village, making it easy for us to locate our destination. Saint James, named after the patron saint of pilgrims, was originally a simple, small chapel built several decades before the apparitions began, but the building began to sink on the unstable foundation. So as the church leaders found another location and began to draw up plans for a new, safer church, they felt led to build one that could contain nearly two thousand people. Although the parish serves five small villages in the surrounding area, the number of parishioners could never have filled the building's capacity. But they felt God's strong impression to build something larger than would serve their simple needs. After the apparitions began, some actually occurring inside the church in a room just to the side of the altar, the parish members understood why. As more pilgrims came to Medjugorje, the church began to fill to capacity, even overflowing. Now each hour it holds mass in a different language throughout each day.

I felt such peace every time I entered this simple, sacred place, as though I could feel God's presence there waiting for me. The church was so full every day it was difficult to find a place to sit, so Tom, Anne, and I would often just stand in the back. I liked taking in my surroundings as I waited for mass to begin. I particularly enjoyed viewing the stained-glass windows along the sides high above the pews. Each window depicted a scene that had happened in Medjugorje, such as Mary talking to the six kids.

The service just before the English mass was for the German-speaking pilgrims and the one following ours was for the Italians. As we arrived daily to the church, the German-speaking pilgrims would exit and then we would enter. But the Italians were not as patient and many refused to wait. It was not uncommon to return from receiving communion to find an Italian sitting in someone's seat! They pushed their way in, even though our service had not yet ended. I saw one Italian woman walk right up to a man kneeling in prayer, grab him by his arm, and lift him out of the pew to take his seat. The man was stunned.

After several days of this behavior, I became angry by this show of disrespect. Such rude behavior—especially in a place of prayer! One day I mentioned it to a priest, who smiled and suggested that I look at it from Christ's point of view. All Christ saw was a group of excited people eager to get to mass and pray. Think of how much joy it must bring him, the priest said. As I reflected on what this priest had taught me, I no longer became irritated by the pushy Italians, but actually began to enjoy their antics—even though I still thought it was rude.

After mass, we would do one thing together as a group, such as tour the village, hear a lecture about the history of Medjugorje, or climb Apparition Hill or Cross Mountain while praying the rosary as a group. Then the rest of the day was ours to do with as we pleased. We could pray or shop or grab a cup of cappuccino. That was a great time to people watch. While most folks appeared fairly normal, there were the odd birds. It seemed as if everyone saw Mary's image in or on something. Someone would point out a rose and say it was in the shape of Mary. One woman in our group picked up a rock off the ground and glued it on her nametag because it looked like Mary to her.

When I saw it, I mentioned obviously, "You have a rock on your nametag."

"I know. Isn't it beautiful? Looks just like Mary."

Later when I told Tom and Anne that story, we had a good laugh at the craziness of it all. Anne, who was eating an apple, took a bite and then she inspected the area she'd bitten. "I don't know," she said. "I think I see Mary in there. Do you see that?" She held it up to me.

"Absolutely."

We weren't trying to be sacrilegious! There was just so much to take in and so much humanity to deal with, and our laughter lightened up the experience.

These were, in a sense, group-bonding times. I connected with a group of women from Cincinnati. Their husbands had taken this trip several months earlier in October and it was now their turn to enjoy Medjugorje. The women were full of life and laughter and everyone enjoyed having them around. In particular one of the women intrigued me. She was everything I was not: she was a good Catholic mom. I listened in amazement as she spoke of her children and their family life. She would sneak into her children's rooms at night to bless them with holy water. They lit a blessed candle together when any of them needed help with a difficult test or had a special need. She had everyone doubled over in laughter as she related how one time she frantically tried to pin a holy medal on her son without his knowing as he headed out the door to his prom. I was simply in awe of her. I had a difficult time believing I could ever be a mother like that. But I knew I wanted to try.

I also enjoyed spending time with Jim. After that experience together our first night, I wanted to learn more about him. Specifically, I wanted to know if he was for real. I found him to be humble, a man filled with peace and incredible joy. He had a terrific sense of humor and loved to tell stories. Jim confided to me that he was not much of a religious man when he first visited Medjugorje. He had gone with his wife and several of her friends simply to "carry the luggage and take care of the women." He had no interest in what was happening in this place. But one day as he was kneeling next to his wife in Saint James Church, he looked up at the altar at the front of the church and noticed a small ball of gold light bouncing around where the bread that had been blessed and believed to be turned into the body of Christ was kept. Next the ball of light moved to the front wall just right of the altar. Suddenly it disappeared and in its place Jim saw the crucified body of Jesus. He noticed pieces of his beard had been actually torn out from his face, and he was beaten so badly that he was almost unrecognizable. Just as suddenly as it had appeared, the beaten image of Jesus was gone. Since that moment, Jim seemed to have been given certain gifts. He noticed when he prayed with people, Jesus sometimes healed them and he seemed to receive messages from Mary and Jesus as well. While this was pretty difficult stuff to grasp, I found myself slowly believing him, but being more of a scientific, you-have-to-be-able-to-prove-it kind of person, I continued to observe him closely.

The trip was proving to be much more than I'd even anticipated. I enjoyed spending time with the group, praying, and investigating the village and its surrounding areas. But we still hadn't experienced one of Mary's apparitions.

One night while eating a late dinner at Vicka's house, we learned Ivan, another one of the visionaries, was scheduled to have his apparition with Mary at nine o'clock on Apparition Hill and it was going to be public. Most of his times with Mary were private but every once in a while, he would have a public apparition time. Excitement coursed through the group as we realized we had an opportunity to be present for this sacred moment.

We quickly finished eating, grabbed our flashlights, and eagerly headed to Apparition Hill. We thought that by leaving for the site at around seven o'clock that would give us more opportunity to get closer to the top, and closer to Ivan. But as we got nearer to the place, it was apparent everyone else had had the same idea. I felt like I was in a herd of cattle! Thousands of people from every different nationality were swarming and shoving to get the same access to the Blessed Mother as we wanted. We forged our way as high as we could get—about a quarter of the way up the hill and behind the blue grotto area where I'd smelled the roses on that first night, and then we held our ground. People were pushing on us from all sides, and all around us, we could hear a cacophony of rosaries prayed in every language possible, with each group trying to pray louder than the next. Some were actually screaming their Our Fathers and Hail Marys. Finally I couldn't help myself and began to laugh aloud.

"I feel like we're in the middle of the War of the Rosaries!" I told Tom and Anne.

Soon people around us began to pass items—mostly small things such as rosaries and crucifixes—up the hill from one group to the next.

"Why are we passing these up the hill?" I asked, feeling ignorant, as though I should know this already.

Jim smiled kindly. "They pass these up for the Blessed Mother to bless." He explained that whenever Mary appears she gives her motherly blessing to everyone present and blesses any religious articles. (Mary always requests people to have their articles blessed by a priest in addition, because her Son's blessing is the most important one.)

I thought that was a nice idea—until I was handed a life-sized statue of Mary and a suitcase bulging with rosaries that had to weigh at least fifty pounds. I couldn't decide if this was a *Seinfeld* episode or Disneyland for religious people.

How will these people ever find their things later on? I wondered and let a chuckle escape from my lips.

Suddenly a hush fell over the crowd. "Be quiet! She's here!" some people yelled at the screaming rosary pray-ers who hadn't realized what was going on. Finally, once the message got through the language barrier, all prayers stopped and everyone was still. Just then as crazy as this scene had been, I had to admit that an indescribable peace and joy flowed through my body. It seemed I could actually feel Mary there. I placed my hands on my stomach, hoping somehow to convey this special moment to my baby.

The stillness lasted about ten minutes and then she was gone. Immediately, people began to surge toward the top of the hill to recover their items, while others tried to make their way down the hill in the now darkness of the night. I felt myself pushed and pulled along the rocks. I tried to hold my flashlight out to see where I was stepping, hoping I wouldn't fall or slip, but with so many people shoving, I could only step and trust I didn't break an ankle. By the time we reached the bottom, I was exhausted.

Before we'd gotten there, I'd envisioned the apparition to be nice and reverent. Even still, afterward in the midst of talking about the carnival atmosphere, I was in awe that I had again been in the presence of Mary with my child. I didn't have to be exactly where Ivan was; just being on that hill meant that my baby was sure to be blessed.

The next morning, following the 10 a.m. mass, Tom and I were waiting for our group to gather at our predetermined spot when I noticed a small group to the right of me pointing at the sky. They looked amazed and some wore huge smiles.

I nudged Tom. "What do think of that?" I said as I pointed at the group.

He shrugged. "It looks like they're looking at the sun."

"Hey, Jim," I said, as he approached us, "what are they doing?"

"They're looking directly at the sun. It's one of Medjugorje's miracles."

"Wait, you look directly at the sun?" Tom said. "You aren't ever supposed to do that, are you? It's bad for your eyes."

Jim nodded. "Normally, yes, but this is a special gift that allows people to look directly at the sun without experiencing any pain or harm. It's just one of the many miracles of Medjugorje. Do you want to try it?"

"Yes!" I answered immediately.

Tom, however, was hesitant. "I'm not so sure. I don't want to risk damaging my eyes."

"You don't just look at it right away," Jim explained. "First, we need to pray."

We all took a moment of silence and I prayed intensely to be given this gift.

After a few moments, Jim said, "Okay, now first stare at the horizon until you see a small disc come up. Once you have that in your eyesight, you can follow it up and over the sun."

I stared into the horizon for what seemed like two minutes. Just when I was about to give up, it was there. A small silver disc had appeared. It looked like one of the host pieces of blessed bread we received at communion. Slowly I followed it up in the direction of the sun. I felt some trepidation, since I was a doctor after all, and I knew how the sun could permanently damage my eyes. I knew it wasn't the most brilliant thing to do, but I wanted to experience everything I could here. Finally, the disc covered the sun and I was able to look directly into the sun's brilliance without any pain. I didn't even squint! I watched it pulsate and dance around the sky as great bursts of flame radiated out from behind the disc.

"Tom, you have got to see this!" I said, not taking my eyes off the brilliant red sun as it throbbed like a beating heart in the sky.

"I don't know, Cyndi..."

"Just try. If you don't see the disc then don't look."

Finally Tom looked into the horizon. "I see it! I see the disc." As he moved up to the sun, he said, "Wow, the sun is dancing all over the sky!" Just then he gasped, and in that moment I saw two beams of light burst forth from the sun to form the shape of a cross.

"What do you see?" I asked him.

"The cross," he replied, his voice filled with awe.

"Me too."

We stood silently and watched as the cross continued to burst forth from the sun and then change colors from red to yellow to blue and purple.

After the disc disappeared, I glanced at my watch. We'd been looking directly into the sun for twenty minutes.

One evening toward the middle of our week, Jim approached Tom, Anne, and me. He looked concerned. "There's a problem with Nancy," he told us. "We need as many people as we can get to join us for prayer in her room."

Nancy was traveling with our group and, like me, she was pregnant.

"What's wrong with her?" I asked, moving into my physician mindset.

"She's cramping and bleeding heavily."

That was definitely a problem. My heart felt heavy as I tried to push back my worst fears for her: I was afraid she was suffering a miscarriage.

When we got to her room, I could sense the deep pain she was feeling. "I'm having a miscarriage," she said. "I've had four before, so I'm afraid it's—" a sob choked off her words.

If that was the case, there was little any of us, including me, could do to help her. But we could pray.

Jim had a metal crucifix that he wore around his neck constantly. Earlier in the week he had shown it to Tom and Anne and me. He'd explained that it contained relics, or small bone fragments, from eight different saints. I'd been amazed since I knew those kinds of relics were not just given to anyone. A person had to have a special gifting to be able to receive something as significant as that. Now Jim removed that crucifix from around his neck and gently laid it on Nancy's abdomen and then he put his hands over that.

"Everybody gather around and place your hands on Nancy," Jim said.

I, along with ten other people, leaned in and placed our hands on her. My hand rested lightly on her lower right leg.

"Mary, bring your Son," Jim prayed. "Jesus, we ask for your presence here. We ask that you heal Nancy entirely, completely, that you save the baby, that you stop the bleeding and the cramping." He continued with his requests and finally said, "Let's everybody say an Our Father, Hail Mary, and Glory Be."

Each of us began to pray with incredible intensity. My prayers came from a point of knowing what it was like to miscarry a child. I'd had a miscarriage right before this pregnancy, so I knew that physical and emotional pain intimately. The emotional agony could better than match the physical pain. As I prayed, I felt her body grow burning hot.

When we finished our prayers, Jim said, "Man, did you feel how hot she got?" Then he patted the cross on her abdomen. "You keep this and pray with it," he told Nancy.

"It's gone." she said. Her face no longer held its anguished look. She blinked a few times and took several deep breaths, and then smiled. "The pain has stopped."

Everyone rejoiced and praised God for his healing. But I was in shock and could only think, *This is too much for me. This is way too much for me.* I felt overwhelmed by everything I had experienced during my time in this place—from the scent of roses I'd smelled, to the cross disappearing, to the miracle of the sun, and now this. It was all coming at me too fast and it was too much for me to take in.

"Tom," I whispered. "I've had it. I've got to get out of here."

"I've had it too," he said. "Where are you going?"

"I need a drink."

"I'm going with you," he said, and Anne nodded.

We found Johnny's, a little bar tucked away down a quiet side street, and ordered beers.

"I just need a beer," I tried to explain to Tom. "I know I'm pregnant. I don't really believe it hurts the baby just to have one single beer. So that's what I'm going to do if you guys are okay with that."

"It's fine," Anne told me. "Go ahead. I think I'm going to need more one just one."

As I nursed my beer, I finally blurted out what I'd been thinking for the past week. "You know, I really can't handle much more. I've seen things. I've experienced things way more than I could have ever imagined. But this healing thing is just too much for me."

When I first came on this trip, I knew I'd wanted to take in as much as I possibly could, but this felt like God had opened a fire hydrant and was asking me to catch all the water in my mouth. It was impossible!

The next day Nancy told us that the bleeding had stopped. She checked as soon as everyone left her room. She should have had a miscarriage. She should have been wiped out and barely able to move. The emotional toll should have been too much for her. But that morning, she came to breakfast looking radiant. "I've been healed," she said. "The pain was excruciating. I was afraid I'd lost the baby."

I nodded my understanding and hoped she was right. I knew deep down, she'd been healed, but as a physician, science simply has no explanation for what occurred, so I still battled internally between what I'd experienced and what my brain told me couldn't be true. It turned out science could never explain what faith had accomplished. (After we returned stateside, Nancy visited her obstetrician, who informed her that she was in perfect health. She went on to have a healthy baby boy.)

Later that day while the group was still talking about what had happened, Jim explained, "Oh yeah, when people get healed, I can feel them. They get red hot. She got red hot." What he'd said was true. I'd felt that heat on her. The only explanation I could come up with was that the Holy Spirit was washing through her and healing her, and that the heat was the presence of God.

Before we knew it, the week had come to an end. I felt as if I'd received a graduate-level training in my faith, and my brain simply couldn't take another event. Even so, I was sad to leave. This place had been a haven for me—even as overwhelming as everything had been. Now I had to go back to my everyday life. I wondered how my life and faith would change after this Medjugorje experience. And of course, I wondered how that faith would play out in the midst of everything I knew about science. I was soon to find out.

PART 3

Kelly

CHAPTER 11

It's a Girl!

I arrived home to three happy boys and my husband waiting for me at the airport. I scooped up my sons, grabbed Drew, and gave them all a huge hug. They all wanted to know how my trip had been. As we loaded my bags into our minivan and headed home, I told them all about the background of Medjugorje, the schedule of everything we had done, as well as some of the antics I had seen, but I didn't mention the miracles I had experienced. Drew didn't press me for more information, and honestly the boys wouldn't allow it. They were so busy filling me in on everything that had transpired while I was away. Apparently we now had a pet snail named Johnny, and I just had to see it! I smiled to myself as I listened to all their adventures. I was finally home and loved jumping back into the family scene.

As we tucked our boys into bed that night, Drew tried to bring up the trip and ask questions about my time there, but I added little to what I had already shared. My experiences were between God and me, I reasoned. Besides, how could I explain to Drew all of what I'd experienced if I couldn't really wrap my own head around it? I believed in everything I had witnessed, but it was beyond explanation. So I opted instead to keep them all hidden in my heart.

I'd taken trips before where they'd made such a great impression but then once home and back to my daily routines, the wonder and awe of the experience faded. I didn't want that to happen with this trip. I was filled with peace and joy and I didn't want to lose that. The funny thing was that for most of the week in Medjugorje, I thought the reason I felt so good inside was because of their coffee! I kept thinking, *Wow, their coffee is* really *good.*

Although the coffee *was* wonderful, I began to realize that it was not the caffeine, but the Holy Spirit who filled me with such joy. That inner peace and completeness I felt didn't have to fade away with the return of my daily routines. I just needed to keep my prayer life up, and the Holy Spirit would remain in me through them all.

Once home, I found my faith continuing to deepen and the love I felt for Jesus becoming more immense. I began to fully live Mary's requests. I prayed the rosary daily, I began to go to confession once a month—and it was not as terrifying as I had imagined. Instead I found the priest to be warm and understanding. I had even found a wonderful Bible study. I'd always wanted to read the Bible, but I didn't even know where to begin. How do you just pick up a Bible and start reading? I wanted somebody to tell me what was going on in the Bible and walk me through it. And I found a study that did exactly that. It was an answer to prayer.

Since the Blessed Mother asks that we give up something we love on Wednesdays and Fridays, I committed to fasting on those days. Being pregnant, I wasn't sure I should fast from food, so I gave up something much more difficult for me: listening to the radio. I loved to fill my day with music. It had been a major part of my life since I could remember, so that felt like a good choice. When that fast became easier, I gave up watching television, which I knew would be even *more* difficult—especially on Friday nights when *West Wing* kept me glued to my seat (and we didn't have a DVR or Netflix back then, so what I was missing, I was *really* missing).

But slowly, that too became easier. As the kids and Drew would watch their programs, I would quietly exit the room and involve myself in other things as I silently prayed and tried to keep my focus on Christ. Soon I noticed a silence begin to enter my life. My mind was no longer constantly filled with images and melodies from what I had watched or listened to. Now my mind and heart were more open. Mother Teresa once said, "In the silence of the heart, God speaks." God does speak to us, but very softly and very gently. When I kept myself busy all the time and my mind filled with noise, I was unable to hear him. Now I was attentive to those gentle urges and whispers I heard in my heart. I didn't realize how important this would become in my life.

In the midst of my spiritual growth, the baby inside of me was growing nicely as well. All my check-ups were normal and the boys were constantly rubbing Mommy's tummy and wondering whether this baby would be a sister or another little brother for them. Drew and I wanted the gender to be a surprise to all of us, as we'd done with our other children. We had our names picked out: Luke for a boy and Kelly for a girl. We laughed at the thought of ever having a girl, though, since Kelly had been our choice for a girl four times running now. It seemed as if boys were the only thing this family would be filled with.

Although Drew and I really did want a girl, the most important thing for us was to have a healthy child. I did all the "right" things—eat well, exercise, practice the best medical care. I'd seen and heard of children who were born with disorders and the pain their parents had suffered through it. One morning while in the shower, that thought entered my brain and I briefly wondered what I would do if this babe in my womb weren't perfectly normal and healthy. It stunned me since that was the first time I'd ever even considered such a prospect. I realized I'd never even thought my children *could be* anything but perfect. A sickening feeling washed over me as I said aloud, "God would never ask that of me. I couldn't handle it."

But a small inner voice replied, *Yes, you could.*

I shook my head to clear it, thinking the hormones were just getting the best of me. I was ready to have this baby. All signs were good. I was just being overly imaginative and emotional.

As with my previous three pregnancies, this baby was late. With each day past the due date, my obstetrician monitored the baby to ensure there were no signs of distress. But after two weeks of this and no signs of progression into labor, my obstetrician decided it was time to induce it. So on December 2, 2001, I entered the hospital, and I couldn't have been more grateful. I was so uncomfortable; I wanted that baby to be born yesterday!

The medical team inserted an IV into my arm and started me on Pitocin, the synthetic form of the hormone oxytocin, to induce contractions. After a few hours, I began to have small contractions that eventually grew stronger. Soon I received an epidural, and then several hours later, I was in full-blown labor. I couldn't wait to see this child, even though I was certain it was a boy. I knew Drew would be ecstatic and that all I was going to hear were jokes about how we were starting a basketball team.

"Cyndi, it's time," my doctor told me, as nurses prepped the room to begin the official delivery. With my doctor's guided encouragement, I pushed. Soon I heard the gentle cry of a newborn fill the room and I held my breath in wait.

"It's a girl!" my doctor announced.

I didn't believe him. It simply wasn't possible. I'd hoped for a girl, but my track record was boys all the way. I looked to Drew for confirmation. If my obstetrician had been joking, I'd see the truth on Drew's face. His face held the brightest smile I'd ever seen.

"It's true, Cyndi," he told me. "We have a girl."

Just then I got a glimpse of my baby as the doctor handed *her* to the nurses to be examined and washed. I was incredulous. It *was* a girl, but how could this be?

And then I knew: She was a gift from God. He had given me everything I had ever wanted. I had my faith, my career, my family... and now I had my girl.

"I'm so proud of you, honey," Drew whispered in my ear. "I've always wanted a girl." Hearing him utter those words put my heart to rest. *I'd* wanted a girl, but I was always concerned that he had just gone along with my confessions to be kind but that he had truly wanted another boy. Now I knew that wasn't the case. We both had received this amazing blessing, and we were overjoyed.

After they checked her over, cleaned her up, and wrapped her in a soft, warm blanket, a nurse placed my little female bundle in my arms. The first thing I noticed was her beautiful, ruby-red lips, like a rosebud that offset her pale skin.

"She's perfectly normal," the doctor told me.

I hugged her closer to my chest. Our precious little girl, Kelly Elizabeth, was fine.

You are so good, God. Thank you for this wonderful treasure, I silently prayed.

The first couple weeks with Kelly at home were like that of any other family with a newborn. A continuous whirlwind of diaper changes and never-ending night feedings were all piled on top of our regular routines and schedules. Everyone had to find their new place in the family.

It seemed to be hardest on my three-year-old Jack. He was frustrated enough that this new baby was taking his place as the youngest, but on top of that, he had to compete just to hold her. Jack had loved being the little brother, so he wasn't too sure he liked this change of events. Plus he always wanted my attention. "Put the baby down!" he'd often say, as he tugged at my hand to have me run and play with him.

My middle boy, John, was five and adored Kelly. He'd hold her constantly, if I'd let him. Whereas my oldest, Drew, who was seven, seemed content simply to hold her hand.

The most fun member of the family to watch interact with Kelly, though, was Drew. He was so proud of his little girl. He hated to leave her in the morning and would rush home from work, run inside, and scoop her up into his arms. Then he would place her in the stroller and off they went to visit every neighbor so he could show her off.

Kelly was truly a beautiful baby and very sweet natured. Like her brother Drew, she was fair skinned with fine, blonde hair that fell into gentle curls. Her soft blue eyes were always curious, watching whatever was going on around her. She smiled easily and had a tender laugh that warmed you inside when you heard it. She rarely cried, and was content to be in her bouncy seat while I ran about the house taking care of the daily chores. But the minute her dad returned home, she was in his arms and there she stayed the rest of the night.

My treasured time with her was during the day when the boys were at school or outside playing and Drew was at work. I'd spend hours just gazing at her, dreaming about all the fun things we would do as mother and daughter.

A few weeks after Kelly was born, I began to notice that something about her seemed different from the boys at that age. Her shoulders and upper arms looked as if they were rolling inward toward her chest. She never moved them and she didn't hold up her head. I reassured myself by insisting it was simply a developmental delay, and didn't give much thought to the fact that Kelly never wrestled or squirmed out of her blankets. I thought she was so gentle because she was a girl. The obstetrician and Kelly's pediatrician had both said she was normal, so I figured that it would resolve itself as she grew older.

When two months had passed and she still wasn't jostling around as the boys had at that age, I continued to tell myself it was nothing to be concerned over. But then one day Drew came home from work looking pale and sick with worry.

"Drew, what's wrong?"

"A patient came in today with a two-month-old baby..." he started to explain as he looked at Kelly. "This woman's baby looked nothing like Kelly."

"Is the child okay?" Perhaps the baby was sick, I thought, and that was why Drew was upset.

He shook his head. "The baby was so strong," he said quietly. "She was holding her head up and moving around all the time."

Suddenly I felt sick inside; I knew what Drew was getting at. It wasn't the woman's baby he was worried about. It was ours. We both looked at Kelly. She was smiling sweetly at us in her bouncy seat, with her arms gently lying at her side.

Images from the past two months flashed across my brain. She'd never flailed or even moved her arms or shoulders, only her hands. And she couldn't hold her head up. I could no longer ignore what was now blatantly in front of me: Kelly wasn't developing as she should, which meant something was terribly wrong with her.

CHAPTER 12

Searching for Answers

Everything within me wanted to deny what was right in front of me. The thought that something could be wrong with my sweet daughter was beyond what my mind could take in. This was my baby who was with me when I experienced all those miracles and was even visited by the Blessed Mother. She was born perfectly normal, so there couldn't be anything wrong with her!

But I also knew we needed to get to the bottom of this issue. Deep down, I hoped it was something simple that science could fix. Or something that she'd grow out of. It couldn't be too serious. That was the mother side of me. The physician side, however, knew that it probably wouldn't be a simple fix.

Kelly was scheduled for her two-month checkup, which was a few days away, so I decided to bring it up then. When I described

Kelly's symptoms and expressed our concerns, the pediatrician seemed genuinely surprised.

"Really? I didn't see anything at her last visit," he said. "Let me take a look at her." He turned to the exam table where Kelly lay smiling, wearing only her diaper. As I looked at her, a knot came to my stomach. I realized for the first time that I had never been afraid she would roll off the table. She had always stayed exactly where I'd left her.

The pediatrician looked down at Kelly, who gently smiled up at him and followed him with her eyes.

So trusting, I thought, and swallowed hard to keep from becoming emotional.

He gently lifted one arm, moved it in all directions, and checked for reflexes. Then he worked with her other arm, and then moved to her legs. I couldn't tell what he was thinking as he worked each limb. Finally, he held each arm above her head and let go. Thud. Each arm fell to her side like a mallet. My heart broke.

"I see what you mean," he said. "She is definitely weak. I think we better get that looked at."

"Drew really wants her to go to an orthopedic guy to check out her arms," I told him.

"Okay, let's do that. But let's have her see a neurologist too, because she isn't really moving her legs either."

My mouth dropped open slightly. He was right. I'd been so focused on her arms that I had never bothered to look at her legs. How could I have failed to notice? I felt like an idiot. "But they move," I protested feebly.

"Yes, but very weakly. I can't find any reflexes in them. Maybe a neurologist has seen this before, but I haven't."

He made a few notes for Kelly's file and then left the room, our appointment finished. I sat and looked at my baby.

Great, I thought. *Just perfect*. Not only did he fail to give me any help, but he had suggested her diagnosis was worse than I'd originally figured. *It's her entire body. What is going on with my daughter?*

We needed to find out. And that meant I was about to enter the world of medicine and its harsh and chaotic system of endless doctors and evaluations and guesses—only this time as a patient's mother.

I scheduled both appointments and a few days later Kelly and I sat in the pediatric orthopedist's office at Children's Hospital in San Diego. Drew had wanted to come with us but couldn't get out of his work appointments. I didn't push too hard since I was a doctor and I could handle the situation—or so I figured.

As soon as the doctor entered, I could tell he had a kindness about him, but I could also tell he was clueless. He took one look at Kelly, furrowed his brow, and said, "Let's take some x-rays."

X-rays seem to be the go-to test when doctors don't know what else to do. I agreed to the x-rays of her shoulders and arms, but when he also recommended one of her hips, I said no. I didn't want to expose her reproductive organs to x-rays.

"Do you *really* need a pelvic x-ray?" As I expressed my concerns, he looked at me as though he were thinking, *You don't have to worry about that. That's not even going to be an issue with her.* As though he believed she had bigger problems for me to worry about.

As I watched his face and continued with my concerns, I panicked. I'd given looks like that to patients too. I knew what the look meant: there was something *seriously* wrong with Kelly. He may not have known what it was but he knew it was severe.

I nodded slowly. "All right. If you need it, go ahead." But I was sick about the fact that she was going to be x-rayed there.

When the x-rays came back, he positioned them on the lighted wall and looked them over. "Well, her x-rays are totally normal. And physically, developmentally she's normal. Her bone structure is completely normal. I don't know why she's not moving, but I do know the reason her shoulders are rolled in is because her pectoralis muscles aren't fully developed. But I don't know why that is."

I groaned inwardly. "So what does that mean? What's wrong with her?"

He shook his head. "I have no idea. I'd recommend that you see a neurologist."

"I've already made that appointment. Isn't there something, some indication, some educated guess you can make?"

He shook his head again. "I'm sorry, no." Then he made his notes and exited the room, again leaving Kelly and me alone.

I was crushed. I wanted him to have the answer for us. Not only did he not give me an answer, he gave me the distinct impression that this was serious enough that whatever it was, it wasn't going to be diagnosed and treated and then over. Then my blood began to boil. Why was this so difficult? I needed someone to tell me what to do to fix my daughter, but no one was helping. And no one seemed all that concerned or interested to fight to get to the root of the problem. Instead they were, little by little, only taking away any hope I had. Why wouldn't they just say that she would be all right? I really needed someone to tell me she would be fine. And why couldn't they give me a diagnosis?

A few days after that, we arrived at the pediatric neurologist's office for our appointment. Once in the exam room, I placed Kelly on her back on the table and undressed her. And then we waited. After fifteen minutes or so, I didn't want Kelly to get cold, so I picked her up, laid her in my lap, and began to play with her.

After waiting thirty-five minutes, the neurologist entered the room and introduced himself, with no apology over how long we'd had to wait.

"So what's going on with Kelly?" his tone seemed brusque, almost as if we'd interrupted his day.

"She's not really moving her arms or her legs."

"How does she do on her stomach?"

"I haven't ever placed her on her stomach. I—"

"You've never put her on her stomach?" His sharp tone sounded as though he really meant to say, "Are you kidding me? Are you some kind of a moron?"

"Kelly wouldn't be able to handle it," I told him. "She can't even hold her head up. So I'm afraid she would suffocate if I did something like that."

"Bring her over here and put her on her tummy." Again, his tone conveyed that he thought I was some silly, overly worried mom who didn't understand anything about children.

Knowing he would not be content without doing this test, I placed my little girl on her tummy and watched as she lay there like a rag doll, unable to move and barely able to breathe.

"Whoa, whoa, whoa. Pick her up. Pick her up."

"See?" I said. "She cannot move. Do you understand?"

At that point, he became much more professional—since now, obviously, I wasn't as silly as he'd figured and I clearly wasn't wasting his time. But it was too late for that with me. I felt the frustration rise within me again. I knew in my heart he didn't know what Kelly had. And I didn't appreciate being treated that way.

"Let me take a look at her." He placed her on her back and examined her the same way the other doctors had, testing for reflexes and lifting her arms and legs. "I'm going to order some tests: a CT scan, some blood work, and a muscle biopsy. That will give us a better idea of what we're dealing with."

Drew joined us when Kelly was scheduled for the CT scan. Her big blue eyes gazed up at Drew and me and she gurgled and smiled as she slowly entered the scanner. Her results came back normal.

When the technician pricked her arm to get a blood sample, she let out a soft, gentle cry. That test also came back normal.

Next was the muscle biopsy. As the moment came closer for the procedure, I refused. I couldn't do it. I *wouldn't* do it. I knew it was typically a very painful procedure, and before I would put my daughter through that, I wanted to see someone else. I needed a second opinion because I didn't think this doctor knew what he was doing, and I had lost all respect for him after he had treated Kelly and me the way he did. Drew agreed, and we left to figure out our next option.

By this point I hated going to doctors because every time I went they just made things worse. Nobody told me, "It's fine. She's going to be better. It's just developmental delay." That's all I wanted to hear. But everybody kept acting like this was a serious problem.

Several days later, a friend referred me to a pediatric neurologist who was one of the best in the country, and—as providence would have it—she practiced in San Diego. I couldn't wait to see her. Her next available appointment was on Valentine's Day, only a few weeks away. I booked it at once and then waited what seemed like an eternity.

The holiday of love arrived and Kelly and I found ourselves once again in the doctor's office. Although Drew had wanted to accompany us, his schedule again wouldn't allow it. But I knew he shared my hope that this doctor would finally help us figure out what was wrong with Kelly.

Dr. Trauner was a warm woman with a quiet strength about her. As soon as she entered the room and interacted with Kelly, I knew that she would be able to help us.

"I understand you have concerns about your baby." Her tone was warm and sympathetic. She was professional and treated me with respect, and I immediately felt more relaxed by her gentle manner.

She knows what's wrong with her, I thought. I just felt it. A seed of hope began to sprout again within me. Then she sat across from me and looked directly into my eyes.

"I know Kelly has gone through a lot of tests. But I want to order one more," she said. She must have sensed my tension because she explained, "It's a blood test and will take the place of the muscle biopsy."

My own muscles relaxed a bit.

"This test is very specialized, and it will take almost two weeks to receive the results. Once we have those, I will need to see you again. This test will likely confirm what Kelly has, but we have to wait for the results."

For the first time in months I felt hope. Even though she'd explained the official diagnosis might not come for weeks, I could tell by looking at her that she knew what Kelly had, so I couldn't leave without probing further.

"What do you think my daughter has?"

"Cyndi, I don't want to even get into it until I have the results in my hands. But you must know that the test is for something very serious. Let's wait until we have the results."

As quickly as the hope came, it fled. I nodded and silently told myself to hold it together at least until she left the room. I gently picked up my baby and hugged her to my breast. So sweet, Kelly limply nestled against my body and looked up innocently at me. With tears threatening to spill over onto my cheeks, I vowed that I'd never again go to a doctor's appointment alone.

I stepped into the lobby and went to the desk to schedule the blood test. As I waited my turn, a man dressed in a tuxedo and carrying a rose entered the office and approached me, flashing a wide smile.

"Are you Mrs. Peterson?"

I could barely respond that I was.

Just then two more men in tuxedos appeared from around the corner and explained they were there to deliver a singing telegram from my husband. He wanted to wish his two girls a Happy Valentine's Day.

As the first man handed me the rose and the trio began to sing, I found a seat in the waiting area and placed Kelly on the chair beside me in her car seat. It was so sweet and thoughtful of Drew to surprise me with this—and I knew he meant it as an encouragement, to let me know that we'd be okay—but as they performed their lighthearted song, all I could do was cry. I thought I could handle all the appointments and tests and run-around, but I couldn't. I'd lost hope for my daughter. And I wasn't sure how much more I could take.

CHAPTER 13

The Diagnosis

*B*reathe, I told myself as I sat across from Dr. Trauner and waited for Drew to show up. He'd promised to rearrange his work schedule to be there with me, to be there for me.

The two weeks of waiting after Kelly's blood test had passed at a snail's pace. Every day I prayed for Kelly to be healed—although I still didn't know of what. But mostly I kept telling myself, *This can't be happening. Not to us. Not to Kelly. God would never allow something terrible to happen to my child.*

Now the moment had finally arrived. The months of waiting and longing to discover what was wrong with our baby had brought us to this place. I sat and forced myself to remain as outwardly calm as I could, trying to make small talk until Drew arrived.

Finally, a light knock on the door and Drew entered, all smiling and lighthearted. "Hey, what's going on? Hi." He nodded to the doctor as he scooped Kelly off the exam table and into his arms and nuzzled her. "Hi, sweetheart," he said and kissed her loudly on her cheek. Then he turned his attention to us. "What's going on?"

Dr. Trauner looked at both of us and my stomach sank. Her face was slightly pinched and her eyes filled with sorrow.

"We have the news on Kelly," she began and then paused as she inhaled. "It isn't good." She paused again. "Kelly has spinal muscular atrophy. I'm sure you've read about it in your search to find a diagnosis for her."

I shook my head. Neither Drew nor I had investigated the situation or assessed the possible diagnoses. We were convinced in the end that this would be some sort of developmental delay and Kelly would be fine. I never researched what this could possibly be, because in my mind it was just like acknowledging that her shoulders were rolling in. If I started to look for something, then she would have something, and I didn't want that. I wanted Dr. Trauner to tell me that everything was fine.

"Spinal muscular atrophy, or SMA, is an autosomal recessive genetic disorder that affects the skeletal muscles," she explained. "Only one in eighty people carry this gene. So in order for Kelly to have acquired this disorder both of you would have to be carriers."

My head started to spin. Drew and I both carried some recessive gene that decided to show up now?

"Obviously, for both of you to carry it is extremely rare," she continued. And then as if reading my mind, she said, "Even then, only 25 percent, or one in four, of that couple's pregnancies will result in this disorder. So you have three normal-appearing children and you have Kelly. And Kelly has the disorder."

I took in a few breaths and then went into my medical mindset. *Okay, this is good. We have a diagnosis. It isn't a great one, but at least we can start the necessary treatment to overcome it. Finally now we can move forward.*

"Okay, so what is the treatment?" I said.

"There is no treatment," she said. "It is 100 percent fatal."

The world stopped spinning.

Fatal.

Just hearing the word pierced my mother's heart. I was sure I misheard. *This is wrong*, I thought. *She misread the test. She got it wrong.* I swallowed a sob and reached over to take Kelly's hand. I gently caressed her and bit my lower lip until I thought blood would seep out. My dreams for this child... everything came crashing down. She would never wear a princess Halloween costume or run on her high school track team. She would never walk across a stage and accept her college diploma. She would never walk down the aisle in a beautiful white gown and say "I do" to the man of her dreams. She would never experience the pains of childbirth or hold her own baby in her arms.

The tears that I'd barely been able to hold back now slipped onto my eyelashes before trailing down my cheeks. I blinked hard. "How long?" I was barely able to ask the question.

"What do you mean? How long until she has problems?" Drew asked me.

"No," I whispered, unable to look at him. "How long do we have until... she dies?"

"Most of these children have an average lifespan of nine months," Dr. Trauner said.

Nine months! My insides screamed. *She's already almost four months old!*

Drew's position in his seat changed. His body became more rigid and he kept rocking Kelly back and forth in his arms. "The test is wrong. Repeat it. We're going to repeat the test."

"No, the test is not wrong," the doctor said firmly. "We are not going to repeat it. I don't want you to go there. You have to deal with this now."

Our last hope was crushed. I sat quietly, taking in the news that I had never wanted to hear and could barely believe.

Now Drew truly grasped the severity of Kelly's condition and began to cry quietly. As he continued to rock Kelly in his arms, he kissed her over and over. Dr. Trauner didn't rush the discussion. Finally, Drew asked, "What will happen to her?"

"SMA is a genetic condition in which a person is unable to use their skeletal muscles. That's because the motor neurons, which give rise to the peripheral nerves innervating these muscles, die in the spinal cord. The nerves leading from these motor neurons atrophy or wither and so do the muscles they innervate."

So basically her muscles waste away to nothing, I thought.

Dr. Trauner remained calm and professional, looking back and forth at us as she spoke. Since we were doctors as well as parents, I knew she would give it to us straight, which I wanted, I needed, to hear. I wanted to know exactly what we should expect.

"There are four types of SMA," she continued. "Kelly has Type 1. It is unfortunately the most severe form and begins in infancy. These children are generally weak from birth and never hold up their heads. They can only initially move their extremities weakly, and over time they slowly lose almost all muscle strength they may have had. Swallowing becomes so difficult for them that aspirating their food and their own secretions become a constant risk. Breathing is also diminished because the muscles between the ribs that aid in inspiration are weak. Since these babies are unable to take in deep breaths, their cough is weak as well. Because breathing is compromised, they have difficulty maintaining the proper exchange of oxygen to the blood, especially at night when they are sleeping."

"What is the cause of death?" It seemed a harsh question, and part of me didn't want to know, but the physician-trained part of me needed to get to the chase—to be blunt and to the point in order to quickly analyze the conditions and develop plans for how I would respond to Kelly's medical needs.

"Pulmonary problems, usually pneumonia. Because the ability to swallow is so compromised, these children will choke on their own secretions, are unable to cough and clear their lungs, go on to develop pneumonia, and die. A common cold can be a life-threatening event because their secretions increase and they have no way to expel them. When she starts having problems, her care will consist of pulmonary therapy and antibiotics."

"How will we know when she needs care?" I was grasping for help.

Dr. Trauner walked to the front of her desk, leaned back on it, and looked gently at us both. "You will know. Now here comes the hard part. You have to take your daughter home with you and go on with your lives." She waited for our reaction.

What she suggested was the most absurd thing I had ever heard. I almost laughed. Kelly needed help. She should be in the hospital. She needed specialists who could take care of her and follow up on her disorder. And she needed that *now*. How could we just leave and act as though everything was as it should be? I felt frantic.

"But who should we go to for medical care?" I asked. "Who will follow her?" I looked to Drew for help. He seemed as helpless as I felt as he continued to cradle Kelly in his arms, gently swaying her back and forth.

"There isn't anything for these children." She explained that we could use the hospital's muscle disease clinics, but they would offer almost nothing for someone with Kelly's condition. "I would be happy to follow Kelly, but really, I recommend that you have your pediatrician track her instead."

My pediatrician didn't even know what Kelly had! How in the world would he be able to follow her? I could not wrap my head around the idea that there was nothing we could do. I'd devoted my whole life to science and this physician was telling me that science had no answer? Nothing at all?

"When should we see him?" I said, still hoping she'd suggest some bit of experimental treatment they could look into or therapy that had worked in special cases.

But her tone remained steady as she replied simply, "At your regularly scheduled check-ups and when she has problems."

"But how will we know when she has problems?" I knew I'd already asked that, but it spilled out without my ability to stop it.

"You'll know. Trust me."

I slowly began to realize that there really was nothing. Nothing to give her. Nowhere to go. Nothing to do.

Nothing.

The situation was hopeless. My eyes turned from Kelly to Dr. Trauner. She had been compassionate throughout the entire visit and I realized then that she would stay as long as we needed her. But with a million questions in my mind and no possible answers, I started to gather our belongings.

I tried to make the tears stop—at least until I could get out of her office. I was at a loss for what to do next. And she was suggesting that we get into our car and drive home. Just like a normal day. Just like every other day leading up to this one. As though the earth hadn't opened and swallowed my soul.

CHAPTER 14

Time to Confess

O utside the building, Drew and I looked at Kelly, smiling happily in her stroller as she looked up at us. We held each other for what seemed like forever. There wasn't anything either of us could say. To be a physician and hear that your child was going to die and that nothing you or science or technology or medicine could do about it was the worst pain I had ever felt.

Nothing. The word screamed at me.

Somehow we made our way to the car and drove home. The depth of my sorrow was more than I could bear. Medicine had failed us. When I needed it most, it had nothing to offer. It had been my rock, my foundation, but now it was crumbling beneath me. Where could I turn? What else was there?

Deep in my heart I knew the answers to those questions. But to respond to them meant that I had to acknowledge the truth to others. Everything in my faith that I'd worked so hard to keep hidden, private, now stood before me and asked if what I believed really was the truth. And if so, how deeply did I believe, what was this faith really worth to me?

Desperation often brings out our character and beliefs in a way other things cannot. And so that night, with Kelly's life hanging between life and eternity, I gathered my strength and courage and sat beside Drew on the living room couch. I couldn't believe what I was about to do, but I had to. Any chance our daughter had for life depended upon it. The fear in my heart was great, but the love for our daughter was greater. Besides, I knew God could heal Kelly; I'd seen him heal others.

I took a deep breath and then released it in a simple sentence. "I need to talk to you."

"I want you to know, I don't blame you or wish I hadn't married you," he said before I could say anything. "We have to be strong and be there for each other through this."

His words took me by surprise and I realized that he probably thought I was going to confront him about our recessive genes— something neither of us knew about or could control even if we had.

"Drew, I don't blame you either. I wish that this had never happened, but not that I had never married you, or that we'd never had Kelly." I took another deep breath. After this confession, I could never go back. "I need to tell you some things that have been going on in my life."

With his full attention on me and with my heart racing, I proceeded to tell Drew everything I had experienced in the last year. I told him about seeing Jesus in the clouds, about the miracles in Medjugorje, about how I was living Mary's requests. I needed Drew to understand that God was real, and that he needed God in his life too, because our only hope for Kelly was a miracle. God was the only one who could help us.

As I finished, I looked into his eyes. "You think I'm crazy, don't you?"

"Why didn't you ever tell me any of this before?"

"Honestly? I thought you would leave me. I thought you would say I was nuts and leave me. I didn't want to lose you."

His face filled with compassion. "Cyndi, I have been married to you for more than ten years. You are the mother of my children. I don't think you're crazy. I love you." He took me in his arms and held me. The relief swept through every vein, every breath. And I wondered why I had waited so long.

We did everything we could think of for Kelly. I gave my notice at the medical practice. I wasn't going to spend one more minute away from her. And then I focused on helping my husband and kids believe in God as I did. We started by praying together as a family. Every night we gathered around Kelly to offer our prayers for her healing. The boys had never prayed before outside of what they did at school or on Sundays at mass. But they were amazing. The prayers that came from their hearts humbled me and I realized how strong children's prayers really are. They are so trusting and pure of heart and have no problem asking for help when they need it. They taught me more about prayer than the prayers I taught them.

In the beginning we simply prayed one Our Father, one Hail Mary, and one Glory Be. The time we spent together in prayer united our family. It brought a routine into our lives, as nightly prayer became a natural part of our day. I let the children fall asleep during our prayers if they were too tired, but we constantly gathered as a family every night to pray.

As word got out about Kelly, our friends and neighbors naturally reached out to help us in any way they could. When they asked what they could do to help, I found myself asking only for their prayers. I wanted to get as many people as possible praying for Kelly. I even went so far as to request that they pray together as a family, because I knew their prayers would be even stronger that way. That was the most important thing they could offer us if they really wanted to help. And they did. I started to receive cards, lots of them, from their children saying how they were praying for Kelly. Many were just pictures they had colored for her, but they touched my heart deeply. The kindergarten and third-grade classes at St. James Academy where John and Drew attended school made books of their prayers for Kelly, and remembered her every day in their morning prayers. One little boy named Rex even began giving up his desserts so Kelly could be healed.

While Kelly's situation quickly spread throughout our Catholic community, local churches and prayer groups of other denominations soon found out about Kelly as well. They reached out in amazing ways, putting her on their "prayer chains," praying for her in their families, and fasting. Several groups came to pray over Kelly while others offered blankets they had made while praying for her healing. I was overwhelmed at the depth of faith I found surrounding me. Before I knew it, I was receiving emails from people all over the country whom I had never met letting me know that Kelly was constantly in their prayers.

Now that the truth of my faith was public, I wanted to go even deeper. I wanted to show God how important he was in my life and that my family was dedicated to him. So I put a crucifix of Jesus hanging on the cross in each of my children's bedrooms. Next I wanted to get our home blessed, but I was so embarrassed that I had never had that done. We had been living in our house for more than seven years and *now* I was going to ask our priest to bless it!

I finally roused up the courage and asked him to join us for dinner one night and then bless our house. I had readied myself to be scolded, but he did not seem shocked at all. In fact he was thrilled by the invitation.

The night was delightful. After dinner he gathered us together and went from room to room sprinkling holy water and blessing each part of the house. The boys all wanted extra holy water in their bedrooms.

Time went on, but Kelly grew only weaker. I became more desperate. Why wouldn't God heal her? Maybe I needed someone more powerful to pray over her. At once my thoughts drifted to Jim, my new friend from our Medjugorje trip. I had experienced his powerful prayers and his gift of healing. So one night after our prayers with the boys, I told Drew about Jim and asked if we should consider having him come to California and pray over Kelly.

"Sure, let's do it," he said. "We need to do everything we can."

The following morning I called Jim and told him the news. I felt comforted as he expressed his devastation.

"Would you please come to Solana Beach and pray over her?"

He was silent for a moment. "I would like to do that very much, but first I need to pray to see if this is what God is asking of me."

I was shocked. How could God not want this? What if Jim said he wouldn't come? What were we supposed to do then? And then he said something that really sent me into a panic: "Give me a couple weeks."

A couple weeks? Did he understand the urgency of this request? She had only nine months to live and we were already halfway there. We didn't have a couple weeks' worth of luxury while he figured out if this was supposed to be his role to pray for Kelly's healing!

I choked back a sob of frustration, thanked him, and told him I'd wait to hear back from him.

The wait was almost unbearable. Every day I willed the phone to ring. I prayed earnestly that Jim would agree to come. When he finally phoned ten days later to say he would make the trip, I was elated.

"Jim, is it better to have more people than just our family when you come to pray over Kelly? Should I invite people?" I thought of asking my friend Martha and some of the other women from the prayer group.

"Get as many people as you can."

"Really?"

"There's power in numbers."

That was all I needed to hear. I went overboard and invited everyone I knew. My daughter's life was on the line. I laughed as I thought of how I had never wanted anyone to know I believed in God, and now I was asking everyone I could think of to come and pray. As I continued to invite and people continued to agree to come, the numbers grew to the point that there was no way I could hold them all in my home, so I contacted our parish and reserved the parish hall for the night. And then I made up flyers and posted them everywhere I could, inviting the entire community to join us.

I also quickly arranged for Jim's travel. The sooner he could get here, the sooner Kelly could be healed and we could put all of this ugliness and mess behind us.

He flew in the next week. We shared a quick meal at our home before it was time to head to the hall. I was a nervous wreck. I had placed so many expectations and so much hope into this evening. I'd worked so hard to get as many people as I could to come. As Drew, Jim, our kids, and I entered the hall, I couldn't believe what I saw. There must have been at least two hundred people! I was overwhelmed by how much people wanted to do something to help. I could feel everyone's love and support. All I could do was say thank you.

As we neared the front, Jim reached over to me and placed his hand on Kelly where she lay in my arms. He broke out into a beautiful smile and whispered to me, "You have no idea how much this baby is loved in heaven." My heart filled with hope.

I took the microphone and thanked everyone again for coming. It meant the world to us. I began the evening by leading everyone in the rosary. Then I turned the night over to Jim. He took off his crucifix, the one containing the relics from the different saints, and placed it on my daughter. He invited everyone to come forward and place their hands on Kelly or on someone who was touching her. The thought of two hundred people all trying to reach over and touch my baby made me uncomfortable, but I tried to focus my thoughts on her healing. As Jim placed his hands on her head, he asked Jesus to come and heal Kelly. I didn't feel her body heat up, as I had with Nancy, but I rationalized that it could have been because of everything else going on around us. Then he asked everyone to pray silently, specifically asking for Kelly to be healed. Silence fell upon the room for five minutes.

At the end of the silent prayer, he opened the service up to others who wanted to be prayed over or who wanted to stand in for someone who needed prayer. A woman in our prayer group asked to stand in for another member of our group, Kathy, who had advanced breast cancer. That person got red hot.

By the end of our time together, we were all drained. We'd done the hard work of moving the heavens with our prayers. Afterward people approached us and asked what they could do to help. My answer was always the same: just pray. Pray with your entire family. Pray for Kelly's healing.

Finally the evening ended and we returned home. I asked Jim to pray once more over Kelly, after which we all went to bed, exhausted. As I lay Kelly in her crib, my heart ached to know if my baby had been healed. I never asked Jim if he felt Kelly get hot. I didn't want to know. I didn't think my heart could bear it if he said no.

Jim left the next day. As the days passed, I kept watching and waiting with anticipation, but Kelly showed no signs of improvement. I couldn't understand—especially since Kathy made a remarkable recovery. I didn't begrudge her that healing, but I wanted *my* child to be healed. Why Kathy and not Kelly—a baby who had her entire life in front of her? Why wasn't God healing this little girl? I had the faith—and I was now talking about my faith to anyone and everyone. God certainly had the power. What more did I have to do to convince God to heal her?

One day as I prayed over Kelly, I began to wonder if I should take her to Medjugorje. I had witnessed healings there. Maybe, I thought, if Kelly were to be healed, the miracle would happen in that place.

I brought up the subject with Drew, who quickly agreed that we should go and we should take our baby. He suggested that our boys could stay with his parents while we were gone. So I immediately called Jim to ask if he knew of any pilgrimages leaving soon. As circumstances would have it, he and two of his friends, Don and Bonnie, were taking their own group to Medjugorje in just two weeks.

I felt comfortable with Drew and me going, but I had doubts about taking Kelly. She was still in okay shape, but if something happened over there, there was no way for me to get her medical attention. But also I didn't want to ever have a regret, especially with something like this. So I asked Jim if taking Kelly made any sense.

"Cyndi, if she were my daughter I would have had her there a month ago."

With that simple phone call, we were added to the roster. My hope had risen again. This was the child who had been in the Blessed Mother's presence. If I went back, Mary could lift up Kelly to Jesus. Surely, he wouldn't deny his mother's request to heal my baby.

CHAPTER 15

Back to Medjugorje

When Drew, Kelly, and I touched down in Split, Croatia, a man named Ivan quickly approached us and introduced himself as our driver. He hurriedly grabbed our luggage and whisked us to his car. Because we were not traveling with the tour group, we'd arranged for a driver to pick us up at the airport and drive us to Medjugorje, where we'd connect with Jim and the rest of the pilgrims, who had all arrived the day before.

All I wanted was to rest for the three hours it would take to get to Medjugorje. The flight had been long and tedious and I knew once we arrived in Medjugorje, we'd be full on in our search for a healing. Ivan, however, didn't appreciate my needs because he took off out of the airport at an Indy 500 pace. The two-lane roads that wound throughout the rugged Croatian and Bosnian coastlines were narrow and winding—and most of them had no guardrails. So one tire over the "shoulder" line meant a possible face-to-face meeting with the rocky sea below. Ivan, undeterred, drove at full speed, constantly shifting gears, and passing one car after another. I glanced over at Drew to see if he noticed anything amiss. His pale face and clenched fists suggested that he was just as nervous as I.

"Excuse me, Ivan." I finally mustered enough courage to speak. "Why are you driving so fast?"

"The three of you have been invited to be present for Vicka's apparition with Our Lady tonight and we're cutting it very close. We need to hurry," he explained as he passed another car and wove dangerously close to the edge of the road.

Suddenly I thought he wasn't going fast enough.

When we arrived at the visionary Vicka's house, I grabbed Kelly and ran inside, remembering each step and room from my last visit. A few people were walking out of Vicka's private residence, talking excitedly. My heart sunk. I was too late.

As I entered the room, I saw Vicka praying individually over members of the group. How I wished we could have made Mary's visitation. Having met and stayed with Vicka on my last trip here, I could see that those holy moments with the Blessed Mother had shaped her. A simple woman in her late thirties, with fair skin and dark hair that she wore pulled back in a ponytail, she radiated joy and peace. As I gasped a sigh over our missed appointment, Vicka glanced up at me. Her eyes held great compassion.

"I'm sorry, but you missed the apparition." She said aloud the words I already knew. As tears filled my eyes, Vicka reached out and lightly touched my arm and then glanced down at Kelly. "I spoke to Our Blessed Mother about your baby. Mary assured me that this child is in her prayers."

I nodded my understanding. I should have been grateful. After all, wasn't that what I'd wanted? But instead of peace, I felt anxious, as though hearing those words from Vicka weren't enough. I couldn't understand my sense of uneasiness about it. Maybe it was because I'd wanted Kelly to be in the room, to be in Mary's very presence.

Vicka must have sensed my concern, because her compassionate smile widened and she assured me that she would continue to pray. In fact, she placed her hands on Kelly and me in an invitation for prayer right then.

As she silently lifted my family up to the Father, I could sense Kelly's peace. She seemed to radiate joy throughout the prayer. Then Vicka opened her eyes and placed them directly on me. It was my turn to be prayed over. I wasn't sure how she would pray for me. I didn't feel that I needed the prayer, because I preferred for all her prayer efforts to be directed toward Kelly.

Again, Vicka closed her eyes. While I wasn't sure exactly what she said since it was silent, I had heard that she prays seven Our Fathers, seven Hail Marys, and seven Glory Bes over people. I may not have known the specifics, but I was certainly aware of the intensity with which she prayed. Her prayer seemed to float over my body and gather around me like a warm blanket. And I found to my complete astonishment that I no longer wanted to pray for Kelly's healing.

I was stunned by the realization and almost literally shook my head to clear it. I couldn't believe it. I mean, that was why we traveled so far. The whole point was to have Kelly healed!

But something was happening in my heart and soul and it was overtaking every nerve, every sense, every inch of my being. All of a sudden, I knew everything would be okay. That I could truly place her in God's hands and know that he wanted what was best for her—even more than I ever could. The only prayer in my heart now was that God's will be done in Kelly's life—and in mine. Of course, I still desired for Kelly to be healed, but more so, I truly wanted God to work in Kelly's life in the way he desired *and* I wanted to be used as a servant of Mary's in her plan for bringing all of her children to Jesus. I began to pray over and over, "Use me. Let your will be done in Kelly's life, but use me to help you in your plan. Use me. Please, use me."

I didn't know what that would look like or mean for my family. But somehow I knew deep down that it was a prayer God *would* answer.

The week flew by and I continued to pray for God to use Kelly's life and my life, while everyone else prayed for Kelly's healing. Drew was able to experience the miracle of the sun. And he and I climbed Cross Mountain one night and prayed together while Don and Bonnie watched Kelly. But mostly we concentrated on praying for our daughter. Unfortunately, by the last day of our trip, Kelly had caught a slight cold. At least, it would have been slight for a healthy baby. For Kelly, it could mean terrible suffering, as her body didn't have the muscle capacity to cough or breathe deeply.

I'd brought a nasal bulb aspirator and some Children's Tylenol, but that was all I had with me. As a physician I'm always amazed by how resilient the human body is, how much stress it can take and recover. But I was not prepared for what happened with Kelly. I didn't realize how truly weak she was. When she contracted that cold, she went downhill fast.

Drew and I took turns suctioning out her nostrils and throat to insure she could breathe. It was a constant battle to keep her air passages cleared and I could tell she was struggling and extremely uncomfortable. As a doctor I was so used to being able to "fix" these types of situations, but I could do nothing to help her. And that made panic within me rise as Kelly became fussier and more irritable.

It made it only worse that this area had no adequate medical care to speak of for a child such as Kelly. We were on our own. And this had been the day I'd been most looking forward to. We were visiting a well-known priest, Father Jozo, who ministered in the parish at Siroki Brijeg, about twenty-six miles from Medjugorje. Father Jozo had been the parish priest of Medjugorje when the apparitions first began. He was also known to have the gift of healing. His touch, accompanied by his powerful prayers lifted up to God, had healed hundreds of people. Drew and I hoped that Kelly would be one of those people.

The reality of that need for healing swam all around us as Drew and I tended to Kelly's rapidly degenerating condition. I had to get her in front of Father Jozo and have him pray over her, but when we arrived we knew Kelly wouldn't do well in the church during his talk. I knew Father Jozo could go on for more than an hour, telling pilgrims about Mary and her role of bringing people to Christ—which meant we could have a long wait inside with a distressed baby who needed constant care.

I really only wanted Father Jozo to pray over her, and I knew the prayer time came after his talk, so we chose to wait outside in the bright sun that blazed down onto the parish's outside courtyard. Drew and I tried to find some shade, away from the crowds of people milling about, also waiting to enter the church.

As we found a spot, a tour guide from another group spotted us and came over.

"Is this Baby Kelly?" she asked.

My stunned response was a simple nod. I'd never met this woman before, yet she knew Kelly?

The tour guide bent down and gently tickled Kelly's stomach. "She's beautiful."

"Thank you. But how—"

"It seems word has spread all through Medjugorje about this precious little one," she said, smiling and now standing again. "My entire group is praying for her. I'll make sure Father Jozo knows about her too." She held up her hand as though telling us to wait, then she disappeared into the church.

Within moments, the tour guide reappeared and hurried toward us, this time wearing a bright smile.

"He already knows about Kelly. Father Jozo knows," she told us excitedly. "He said not to worry, that he would pray over her after his talk."

I couldn't believe she'd done that for us and felt so appreciative. But more, I was surprised that he was familiar with Kelly and her story and that he would pray over her.

Thank you, God, my heart whispered.

Now we just needed to get Kelly in front of the priest. And as the minutes progressed, I began to question if that were even going to be possible. Kelly continued to fuss and fought us as we tried to suction out the mucus. Everything seemed to pile onto my shoulders—the grief, the suffering, the brief time we had left—and I could feel myself starting to fall apart. I had to do *something*.

When I realized Kelly hadn't eaten all day, I became laser focused on getting her some formula. I could at least handle that.

Or so I thought. But I was unable to find any water. The outside fountain was dry and clearly had been broken for quite a while. In my desperation I raced into the church to find water.

My look of panic must have been clear to a nun who'd stepped out of a room and approached me. She spoke no English, so I had to overcome our language barrier—something I didn't have the time or patience for. But fortunately, when she saw the bottle I held, she smiled and indicated for me to follow her.

Water! Cold water to make my baby her formula. I almost cried for joy and relief as I filled the bottle and rushed back out to the courtyard, sure that this would be the magic pill to calm Kelly.

When I reached her, I could immediately tell she wasn't better. Drew was doing his best to continue the suctioning process. I took her limp little body in my arms and placed the bottle, now holding formula, to her lips, encouraging her to take the nipple in her mouth and suck. But she refused.

"Come on, sweetie." I pushed it gently but firmly into her lips, but instead of accepting the nourishment, she wouldn't open her mouth. We were both feeling frustrated by the circumstances.

Finally, Drew touched my arm. "She can't breathe, that's why she won't eat." Her face had blushed a slight shade of blue, so I laid her up against my shoulder and began to pat her back. Then I went back to suctioning.

The knowledge that Kelly could die right here in my arms came crashing into my reality. I tried not to think what the back of my mind taunted me with: *She's going to die.*

I felt lost. I was certain that bringing her to Father Jozo was the key. I knew that she would be healed here. So why would God bring us halfway around the world, within yards of a priest who could help her, if he were going to let her die? My brain simply could not fathom the point or purpose.

The doctor part of me might have been helpless, but the faithful believer and mother refused to lose hope. Drew and I took turns suctioning until slowly she began to regain her color and breathed a little easier. If we ever needed a miracle, it was now.

About a half hour later, the church doors opened. Father Jozo had finished and many of the inside crowd exited into the courtyard. The prayers must have begun so we headed inside with Kelly, who had calmed down and seemed to be better, although exhausted.

As we entered the dimly lit church, I saw people forming a line, which wound its way around the entire periphery of the room, creating a big circle.

There must have been at least three hundred people waiting.

We stepped into the left-hand side of the line at the back of the sanctuary and waited for our turn to be blessed and prayed over. A medium built, olive-skinned, fiftysomething man with dark hair and dark features, whom I recognized immediately as Father Jozo, started on the other side of us and slowly moved from one person to the next, placing his hands upon their heads as he blessed them. I longed for those healing hands to touch my daughter.

Finally, after about twenty minutes, he reached us. He placed his hand on Drew's head and blessed him and then he moved to me. His kind, dark eyes looked into mine and he smiled. Then he looked down at Kelly. She was now calm. And although her breathing was shallow, she was no longer struggling to the same extent as she had been earlier.

"This is Kelly," I told him.

He nodded and continued with his compassionate smile and placed one hand on Kelly's head while he reached over and laid his other hand on my forehead. He prayed silently for a moment and then removed his hand from me and placed it next to his other on Kelly's head. He nodded slightly as his lips moved in prayer. He remained with Kelly for what felt like a full three minutes before he moved on to bless the next two people to his right. Suddenly, instead of continuing down the line, he returned to Kelly, placed a hand on her head and the other on her little belly, and began to pray for a second time. He moved on again and blessed four more people, but stopped once more and came back to Kelly a third time and prayed. I wondered what he knew and what he was praying for. I prayed it was for her healing.

After the service I felt I'd done what I'd come to Medjugorje for: the visionary Vicka had prayed over Kelly and had lifted her up in her prayers to Mary, and Father Jozo had prayed over her not once but three times. Now it really was time to leave the fear, hope, and concern in God's hands and let him accomplish his will. Kelly seemed to do better and Drew and I breathed easier. I believed Father Jozo had healed her. Everything was going to be okay.

So we packed up our things and headed the three hours back to the airport in Croatia. By the time we were ready to board our plane for the long flight home, Kelly's suffering had returned with a vengeance.

CHAPTER 16

A Call to Obedience

It was the longest flight of my life.

From Split, Croatia, we flew to Frankfurt. Kelly wasn't doing well, but Drew and I figured she was well enough that we could make the direct flight from Frankfurt to San Diego. After takeoff, however, Kelly went from bad to worse to dire. I spent the entire time suctioning her nose and throat, trying to clear the secretions so she could breathe. With a healthy child who has a cold, you may suction once and then maybe two hours later, if it's really bad. With Kelly, it was every few minutes.

I had never felt so helpless and frustrated. Kelly couldn't move, so she was unable to fight physically. She was like a ragdoll. She couldn't cough, just gasp and choke. As I held her I could feel her respiratory rate increasing. Her eyes were squinted down and her heart rate was extremely rapid. I could feel it beat against her tiny chest. She was in extreme distress—and we were thirty-five-thousand feet in the air.

Although Kelly was almost six months old, she had never advanced from formula to solid foods because of her difficulty in swallowing. As her cold worsened, she stopped eating altogether, so she wasn't getting the nutrients she needed to help her body fight the virus. She was crying and fussy and inconsolable.

And I kept wondering why this was happening. Why was God allowing this? I had to accept the fact that Kelly wasn't healed. And that was as heartbreaking as watching her struggle. It tore at my heart. And guilt piled on top of it all.

I've done this to her, my thoughts accused me. *It's my fault because I took her all the way over there. Why didn't God come through? I thought he wanted me to go to Medjugorje.*

I felt lost.

How would I handle losing a child? I looked at Drew and could see he was thinking the same thing. Kelly was going to die on this airplane.

"As soon as we land, we need to go straight to the emergency room," Drew told me. I nodded and looked again at this child who now barely breathed. She was totally spent.

Drew alerted the flight attendant that we needed to disembark first to get to the emergency room. She offered to have an ambulance waiting at the gate, but for some reason, we decided to drive Kelly there ourselves.

By the time we landed, I was beside myself. I couldn't think clearly, I could barely keep from crying. I could feel the other passengers' eyes on us as we quickly grabbed our carry-on bags and rushed from the plane. Drew picked up our luggage and we headed directly to the Children's Hospital of San Diego (CHSD).

Drew had called ahead to tell them that we were on our way and to be ready, so as soon as we arrived at the emergency room entrance, medical staff were waiting to take our daughter.

They immediately placed her on oxygen and IV antibiotics and fluids, then the doctors admitted Kelly to the pediatric ward.

"I think she needs to be in the ICU," I blurted out, knowing that they had no experience with children like Kelly. She needed constant care, not care from the nursing staff that had to consider a floor full of other patients as well.

With a tone that suggested I didn't know what I was talking about, one doctor informed me that it was just a cold. "She's struggling a little bit. We'll just put her in the pediatric ward and monitor her."

"No, you don't understand her condition," I pressed. "This isn't just a cold she's battling. We need to move her to the ICU."

"Well, I don't think so," he stated. "We'll schedule respiratory therapy every four hours and that should make a marked difference."

Every four hours? Did they not realize that I'd just spent *every minute* suctioning out her secretions?

I felt powerless and angry. They knew that Drew and I were both physicians. We knew medicine! Even though I voiced my strong medical opinion several times, I was incapable of changing anyone's mind from anything other than them telling me that Kelly was fine.

I wasn't confident that she would be fine, however, so Drew and I stayed close to her.

The nurses placed her on a pulse oximeter, which measured the level of oxygen in her blood. Whenever the level dropped below 90 percent, an alarm would sound, alerting the nurses to check on her. Unfortunately, every time Kelly drifted off to sleep, the high-pitched beeping noise would wake her. Unable to rest, she became only more tired and feeble.

But I did have to admit that after her first breathing treatment, she did improve. They'd suctioned her pretty deep to clear everything out of the lungs, gave her some medication to keep her lungs open, hit her on her back to give her some mechanical physiology treatment, and everybody thought that would be fine.

But Kelly was just so exhausted it scared me.

Drew let some of our friends know that we were home and updated them on Kelly's situation, and later that evening several showed up at the hospital to pray and support us. I was especially touched when one of my friends, whose brother is a priest, brought him with her, since he was in town visiting family. With about twelve people in the room, we held hands and joined in agreement with the priest's beautiful prayer, asking God for Kelly's recovery. I was so touched that this group of people had cared enough to come and support us.

As everyone lingered and talked, the sound of the alarm kept going off. *Beep, beep, beep, beep.* It was driving me crazy—and I knew it was affecting Kelly. Finally she was so worn out that she didn't even wake up when the alarm went off.

"Cyndi, you're exhausted," my friend Kim said.

"I know." It had been three days since I'd last slept.

"You need to go home." I started to protest, but she cut me off. "I'm going to stay with Kelly tonight. If something happens, I'll let you know. But you can't do Kelly any good if you don't get your rest."

She was right. I knew we both just needed to sleep, so I agreed.

Drew and I went home and crashed. Drew's parents were at our house watching the boys, so we knew we didn't have to worry about them. But even though we were both drained, we were back at the hospital four hours later. Drew stayed as long as he could, but had to go to work.

I was alone with Kelly. Now when the alarms went off, nobody came running anymore. So I would gently nudge her to breathe so she could take in more oxygen. Later that morning, a respiratory therapist came to give Kelly breathing treatments and chest physiotherapy to help her eliminate the secretions in her lungs.

"It won't take me long," she told me, "so you can grab a cup of coffee or something while I work with your daughter."

"I'd like to stay."

"I'd prefer that you didn't." She was adamant about not having me in the room. Since I knew there wasn't anything I could do anyway, I agreed and stepped out. But within a few minutes I could hear every buzzer and alarm blaring loudly from Kelly's room. The PA cracked overhead that the trauma team was needed stat and then it announced my daughter's room number.

Immediately I raced back into the room alongside medical personnel from all over the hospital.

Kelly had gone into respiratory distress in which her heart and breathing rates had soared and her oxygen level plummeted to between 40 to 50 percent.

Each person of the crash team was focused on getting her vitals back into normal range, but they were so far out of whack, nothing was working.

Since they knew I was a doctor, they didn't ask me to leave, and I stayed in the corner making sure I could see but not be in anyone's way. As they continued to work with no progress, a nurse looked over at me.

"You need to get out of here."

I swallowed hard and stepped toward the door with her following close behind. As soon as I exited, she shut the door. I heard the loud click and stood alone on the other side—a chasm between my daughter and me—and I wasn't sure that I've ever see her alive again.

I couldn't move, straining to hear any updates, any cause for hope, but the door was thick and I could hear nothing but my own heart pounding in my ears.

God, you have to help us, I begged. *Don't take her now. Not yet. Please.*

I stayed by the door, praying, hoping, barely breathing, waiting.

As I waited and paced beside the door, I contacted Drew's office to let him know what had happened and then I called anyone I could think of to ask them to pray.

Finally, after twenty minutes, the door opened and the team filed out of the room and past me without a word. My heart skipped a beat.

Why won't they look at me?

Then the lead doctor approached me, looking tired and grim. "We've stabilized her, but barely. We've been able to get her oxygen level back to within the low range of normal, but she needs to go to the ICU."

I wanted to hug him and punch him at the same time. I'd told them that piece of information the previous night and no one would listen. We could have avoided this entire situation if they would have taken my concerns seriously. But now wasn't the time to issue a blanket "I told you so." I wanted to get into the room and see Kelly for myself, to make sure she was okay.

In only a matter of moments, they had her prepped and were moving her to the third floor, to the pediatric intensive care unit (PICU), where doctors placed a nasogastric tube down her nose and into her stomach, to give her nutrition without making her actually eat or drink. They also started her on round-the-clock breathing treatments. She continued on the oxygen treatment, still subject to the monitor that would blare its alarm every time her levels dropped below the required amount. To our dismay, the alarm continued to sound. Constantly.

As she continued to struggle for several more days, her attending pediatric physician suggested that we consider placing Kelly on a ventilator, a machine that would breathe for her. They would place a tube down into her lungs that would inflate them mechanically. Neither Drew nor I wanted to take that drastic measure at this stage, unless it was absolutely necessary, because we knew that once children with SMA went on a ventilator, they rarely came back off, since they would give up what little strength they had even to try to breathe.

"Why don't we wait? Let's just wait one more day. Can we wait one more day? Is she strong enough for that?" Drew and I asked.

"Yeah, she can wait one more day," the doctor said.

By the next morning, we were encouraged to discover that she had improved and was stronger. Her heart rate was down, her breathing was better. Her body seemed to have finally fought off that viral infection and secretions were down, so she didn't have to struggle so much. Even though everything started to stabilize, they wanted to keep her in the PICU to monitor her.

Several days later, I was sitting with Kelly and simply rubbing her hand. I loved to hold her hand. She couldn't hold up her head, but she could slightly roll it to one side, and she would look at me and smile. Her big eyes were so full of love. When I looked into them I felt as though she could see right into my soul. It was as though her young, little body had a spiritual understanding and connection with God and she wanted to pass that to me. Just looking into her eyes brought me such comfort. All we had to do was look at each other.

This particular morning, as I held Kelly's hand and just stared at her, a young medical student walked by the room, stopped, and then stuck his head in the doorway as though he wanted to ask me something. I could tell he was still a medical student by the length of his jacket. (You can determine how far in training students are by the jacket length.) His face carried a slight pinched look, as though he was nervous and uncomfortable.

"Hi." Having been in the same position numerous times when I was a medical student, I wanted to reassure him that it was all right for him to come in. I knew that because Kelly's case was so rare, plenty of interns and residents would want to examine her.

"Hi. Um, I wanted... is it okay if I talk to you?"

"Sure. Come on in. Feel free to look at my daughter."

Relief and a slight smile washed over his face.

"You should examine her," I told him. "You'll likely never see another case like this one."

He smiled again and thanked me. "I already examined her earlier. That was a great opportunity. But that's not why I'm here. Actually, I'm here to see you."

"Oh!" I said, dumbfounded. "You want to talk about medicine?" I thought that perhaps he wanted to talk about my field of dermatology.

He started to fidget, picking at the edge of his jacket, and shook his head. Finally, almost guiltily, he said, "Would you tell me about Medjugorje? I've been all over the world—to the Holy Land, to Fatima and to Lourdes, where Mary has appeared. But I've never even heard about Medjugorje. Can you please tell me about it?"

I could feel my face immediately grow hot, I was so stunned. He could have only known about that trip if loose lips had been wagging. I realized that Drew and I were probably the talk of the hospital. The two doctors who took their child to some crazy place to look for a miracle. I looked again into his eyes, and I could see that he was genuinely interested. So then I laughed and got excited that I could share my experience about the place I'd now fallen in love with.

I explained where Medjugorje was and about all the reported occurrences and miracles there. As I shared my experience with him, I heard a distinct voice inside me say, *Give him your rosary.*

It was so clear in my mind that I stopped abruptly and blinked hard. The medical student gave me a surprised glance, and I realized how silly I must have looked. I smiled slightly and then continued with my stories.

Where had that come from? And why was it asking me to give away my rosary? I could have given away anything else, but not that. This was my special rosary that I'd purchased in Medjugorje on my first trip there. It was made of wood and soaked in rose oil so it smelled of roses, a wonderful reminder of my first night in Medjugorje. One of the miracles of that place was that the silver links that hold the rosary beads together would turn gold. And mine hadn't. And that bugged me. It was the only thing I had asked for. The *one* thing I'd wanted. I saw the miracle of the sun and viewed the crucifix spread out from the sun. I witnessed the healing. Smelled the roses. Got a message. I knew that would be enough for most people. But no, I had wanted my rosary to turn gold.

I knew all those mystical things were not meant to be some big show, that they're meant to be like little candy kisses that Jesus throws us to say, *I love you. See? I'm real and I love you and I'm giving you this little gift to show my power and my presence with you.* They're simply reassurances, because there are many of us who are like Thomas. We can hear it, people tell us they believe it, but we're not going to believe until we see. Until, as the apostle Thomas did, we put our fingers into Christ's wounds.

The special part was that now my rosary actually had begun to change. Three of the silver links had turned gold—and I knew that meant that Jesus and Mary were with me in my suffering. It meant they knew about Kelly. That rosary gave me comfort in a time when I couldn't find deep comfort anywhere else.

Now here was this voice telling me to give it away! I couldn't do it. It must be Satan, I reasoned. It couldn't have been Jesus. He wouldn't ask that of me because he knew what that rosary meant to me. Satan would be the only one who would want to take my rosary away.

But that didn't make sense either. I didn't think Satan would really want me to give a rosary to someone so they could pray with it! No, it wasn't Satan.

Give him your rosary. The voice came at me again, this time louder and more forceful.

Why are you asking this of me? You know what this means to me! It didn't make sense. *No. I won't give it.*

I went on with my conversation and made sure I answered all of his questions. I even provided him with several websites to check out. But I did not give him my rosary.

After the intern left, I felt a heavy weight on my heart, as though I'd disappointed my God yet again. I felt guilty, tormented. My whole body carried remorse that I couldn't shake. The truth of what I'd chosen, of what I'd failed to do gripped my heart like a vise. I had denied my God. I had put my feelings and my desires ahead of his wishes. If that man needed my rosary, who was I to deny him?

That night at home as I prayed the rosary with my family, I could hardly look at it. The thing that had brought me so much comfort now brought me deep regret. Just to look at it was a reminder of how I'd stubbornly refused my savior. After God had saved Kelly's life and kept her alive, how could I be so selfish to cling to a rosary? Couldn't God turn *anything* gold? It wasn't about the rosary, it was about my lack of obedience. His mystical gifts are wonderful, but I'd confused the gift with the giver. Jesus gives but tells us not to focus on the gift, but to focus on him and his love. I still had so much to learn and so much growing to do in my faith.

Later that week I took my three-year-old son, Jack, with me to the prayer group at my children's school. During the prayers he began to play with the beads of my rosary, so I handed it to him. Suddenly the rosary broke into pieces in his hands. Jack expected me to be upset, but I took him in my arms and hugged him. I could finally put that rosary behind me. I could go on. I didn't have to look at it every day and be reminded of what a disappointment I had been to God.

A few days later I went to my bedside table to collect a new rosary. I had purchased several in Medjugorje and kept them by my bed. They too were made of rosewood and smelled beautifully. I pulled one out, sat on my bed, and began to pray for strength and for Kelly. Taking care of my daughter was becoming more difficult each day. She required more and more care and yet seemed only to grow weaker.

As I prayed, I happened to glance down at my hands. Every link on the rosary had turned gold. Every single link. Not just three links. I fell to my knees, my throat tight with sorrow.

"God, I'm sorry. I'm so sorry. You have been so good to me and you ask so little. I know that you will always give me what I need. I just need to trust you and do as you ask. Please forgive me. I will never deny you again."

To know that my trust level was so low, even though I knew God existed, was shameful. I didn't trust him the way I should have. And still he remained faithful. He turned the rosary to show me again, to prove again, to remind again, *Cyndi, you can trust me. I'm not going to leave you.*

I lost that rosary a few weeks later, but what I learned was invaluable. God needed to be first in my heart. A material object couldn't be. If I ended up directing too much love toward something meant to bring me closer to God, I was missing the point. Kelly was in God's hands and I needed to trust that and allow that knowledge to comfort me. Material things are just that: material things. How could I expect a miracle—pray so desperately for one—when I couldn't even be obedient with the little things? God and his desires are most important. I learned if I truly want to serve God, I need to do what he asks. If I don't, I miss a great blessing.

I determined never again to pass up an opportunity to obey him. No matter what he asked of me.

CHAPTER 17

More Desperate Prayers

Kelly's condition was taking a toll on me. I'd quit my job to spend as much time with her as I could. After the experience in Medjugorje and the long flight home in which I was certain Kelly was going to die, and then seeing her go into respiratory distress at the hospital where again, I feared she wouldn't make it, my body and mind just couldn't take much more.

I thought I was simply sleep deprived. I longed constantly for one more hour of sleep, my mind was in a continual fog, and I had lost any sense of joy or humor. What I, as a medical professional, should have recognized but failed to was that I'd fallen into a deep depression.

I didn't even understand the symptoms. Why should I? I'd always been able to solve any problem and master any emotion, so it never entered my mind that I would have it.

But one evening ten days after Kelly had arrived at the PICU, a nurse approached me and asked how I was doing. Her calm, sensitive manner made me feel comfortable, but I wasn't sure how to respond. How did she *think* I would be doing? I gave her a vague answer that I was holding up okay and she smiled kindly and handed me a card.

"You know, you may want to go see this doctor," she said.

I glanced at the card. I didn't recognize the name, but I definitely recognized the title: psychiatrist.

Confused, I looked back up at her. "Me?"

She nodded. "I think it would help."

That night I mentioned my conversation to Drew, expecting him to tell me how crazy the nurse was for suggesting I visit a psychiatrist.

"You know, Cyndi, I think you should."

"Really?"

"Just make an appointment."

So the next week I sat across from a psychiatrist who said simply, "Oh yeah, you're suffering from depression." When she offered to prescribe a mild antidepressant, I balked. "Cyndi, you have a difficult road ahead of you with your daughter. The best thing you can do for her is to be fully and emotionally present. There is no way you can do that right now the way you are."

So I agreed to the prescription. As it kicked in, within two to three weeks the fog began to clear and I felt like myself again. My sleep improved and I was better able to manage the day-to-day responsibilities of parenting my other children as well as caring for Kelly.

Finally after fourteen days, Kelly was released from the hospital, but because of her weakened state, she required 24/7 care, which meant I rarely left the house except for necessities. Taking care of her was a full-time job. Actually, it felt more like three full-time jobs rolled into one. Although it took all my energy to attend to her needs, I didn't mind. I knew time was not on our side. At the end of every day, my mind clipped off another page from the calendar. Another day gone. How many more would I have with her?

After about three weeks at home, Kelly was finally in stable condition. She loved to laugh and play with the lightest of toys, as she could hardly raise her hands, and she constantly followed her brothers with her delight-filled eyes. As I had worked full time when the boys were born, I had hired a nanny to care for them while I was at work. Socorro quickly became part of our family and we all adored her. As I cut back on my hours once I was able to, I found I loved the added time Socorro allowed me to have with my boys. As Kelly worsened and required more care, Socorro stepped up and became a godsend for us. She was amazingly good with Kelly and not intimidated by the medical equipment we had at the house. She was as good as any nurse I had ever worked with. So one day while Kelly was stable and in good spirits—happy, eating, calm—I decided to take a break. I needed to get out of the house. Just to replenish and remove myself from the constant fear and worry.

"I'll only be gone a short while," I told Socorro, as though I still wasn't sure I should leave.

"Be gone as long as you need."

As I got into the quietness of the car, I sat for a moment and tried to think of where I could go. Finally a delight passed across my mind.

Nordstrom's.

No one would deny I needed a few new things to wear. This would be the first time I had gone shopping since I received Kelly's diagnosis. I was about to give myself a wonderful treat.

I smiled as I thought about walking through the aisles of clothes and housewares. I could escape my life for just a moment. I pulled into the parking lot and found a great space close to the front. It was going to be a good day.

I entered the building by the men's clothes and walked to the other side of the store to the ladies' department. I found a lovely display of blue tank tops and was sorting through them, looking for my size, when I heard my phone ring from my purse.

Immediately my heart sank. I knew how quickly Kelly could go from good to bad.

I shouldn't have left. I'm so selfish. How could I have left her? I grabbed my phone and answered on the second ring.

"Cyndi? Hi, it's Jim."

"Jim!" Relief gushed into my heart. I hadn't heard from him since our trip to Medjugorje with Kelly.

"How's Kelly?"

I filled him in on her hospital experience and how she was doing now. I didn't want to become emotional in the middle of a department store, so I tried just to give him the facts. But I couldn't help wondering why he had called.

He listened compassionately to my report and then told me he had some news that he thought would interest me. "I know this is late notice, but I wanted to let you know that next week Wayne Weible is coming to my parish to speak."

Wayne Weible? Hope surged again within me. I'd never stopped praying for Kelly—even when she wasn't healed in Medjugorje. But maybe this was the path to Kelly's healing: to have

Wayne Weible pray over her. He had authored the Medjugorje book that fell off the shelf in the Christian bookstore. That book had opened my heart to the knowledge that God truly exists. I had also read that when he prayed over people, they were sometimes healed.

I had to take Kelly to Washington to Jim's parish. I had to have Wayne pray over her.

At Medjugorje I'd felt led to pray for God's will to be done in Kelly's life and had asked God to use me, and I still desired that, but ultimately my humanness led me to revert back to the desperate plea of asking him to heal my daughter. As a mother there wasn't anything I wouldn't do for my child. There was no extent I wouldn't have gone in order to save my daughter's life.

"Thanks for letting me know, Jim. I'll be there."

I could hear the smile in Jim's voice. "I thought you might say that. Don and Bonnie have already offered their house for you to stay at while you're here."

I wanted to throw my arms around him. Since he was two states away, though, I settled for gushing my gratitude.

As I hung up the phone, all thoughts now off the blue tops— and any other shopping—I knew what I needed to do right away. I rushed home to tell Drew the news. Although he couldn't go with me, he encouraged the trip—especially since Kelly was healthy enough again to fly.

I couldn't believe that I was actually more excited for this trip than I had been when we took Kelly to Medjugorje. I knew something big was going to happen.

A week later Jim picked Kelly and me up at the Seattle airport, and drove us to Don and Bonnie's house where we would spend the night. I had gotten to know Don and Bonnie on both of my trips to Medjugorje. They are one of the warmest and funniest couples I have ever met. I loved them and was eager to see them again, glad for the opportunity to spend some extra time with them during this trip. The plan was to have dinner at their house with Wayne and a few of his friends and then head to the parish.

As soon as we walked into their home, a tall, black-haired man in his fifties greeted me.

"Hi, I'm Wayne!"

My mouth dropped open. Here was Wayne Weible standing in front of me with the warmest, humblest greeting. For some reason, in reading his book on Medjugorje, I had begun to think of him as some larger-than-life, superstar celebrity, but I found him to be this down-to-earth, good-natured, normal person who put me right at ease. I couldn't help but like him.

With only two hours before Wayne was to speak at the church, we wasted no time sitting down to eat and getting to know one another. The table held nine of us—Jim's parish priest, Father Gary, Wayne, Jim and his wife, Joan, Don and Bonnie, two women I didn't know, and me. As we sat around the dinner table eating and talking, I listened in amazement to the stories everyone shared about their experiences when Wayne was around. One miracle after another had seemed to happen to this group! If miracles had taken place for each of these people, my faith was fueled by the thought that it was Kelly's turn for a miracle. I knew I'd made the right decision to bring her here.

After dinner, as everyone rose from the table to get ready before heading to the parish, Bonnie asked Wayne to pray over

Kelly. I was grateful when he immediately agreed. Because Kelly had no muscle tone, she would crumple in my arms whenever I'd try to hold her, which would make her uncomfortable and fussy. So I laid Kelly flat on her back on the kitchen table on top of her comfy blanket. Wayne bent over her and smiled.

"You're such a beautiful little girl," he said to her. Her response was simply to smile up at him.

Father Gary moved next to Wayne, as Wayne pulled out his rosary and touched it to Kelly's forehead. Then Wayne began the most beautiful blessing in which he asked Jesus to heal and comfort Kelly and always to keep her in his sacred heart. He called on all of heaven to pray for Kelly's healing.

Although she continued to look at him and smile, she was too weak to do anything else. But I didn't lose heart; I knew that while some healings happen instantaneously, most of them take time and are slow, gradual, persistent healings. I also didn't feel any heat, but I chose not to spend any time pondering that.

As soon as the prayer time was over, we played a bit with Kelly, continued to chat and enjoy our time together, and then all piled into our cars to head to the parish. Wayne gave a wonderful presentation on Medjugorje and reviewed Mary's latest message to the world. He spoke so comfortably to everyone and kept them all enthralled.

He's so at ease in front of people talking about faith. Isn't that funny? He actually seems to enjoy it. And then I thought, *It doesn't really look all that difficult. I think I could do that.* I was surprised by how at peace I felt with that thought and how convinced I was.

Later I mentioned my thoughts to Bonnie. "You know, when I was watching Wayne, I had this thought that I could talk in front of people about my faith."

She stared at me for a moment and then roared with laughter. "Oh, be careful what you ask for!"

She was right, I shouldn't have verbalized it! Now someone could hold me accountable. I wanted to smack myself in the forehead!

That night, most of the group, except for the two women and Father Gary, returned to Don and Bonnie's house to pray the rosary together. I had learned that, when Jim prayed the rosary, at times Mary might speak through him and give messages to those present. Although when I first met Jim, I had been skeptical of his giftings, I no longer doubted. I knew he was obedient to his pastor and the church, that he held himself strictly accountable to his spiritual leaders and remained in close contact with his spiritual director. My skin felt tingly at the thought that Jim was going to pray the rosary with us. Would he have a message from Mary? And more important to me, would he have a message about Kelly? I wanted to know that heaven was aware of her struggle. I wanted the Blessed Mother to keep Kelly in her heart. My head knew that God knew—after all, so many believers had stormed heaven's gates on my daughter's behalf. But my heart, my fragile mother's heart, needed continual reassurance.

We moved into the living room and everyone settled into their own chairs. Some were in oversized, stuffed chairs. Some were on folding chairs. Wayne sat next to the fireplace. I chose to sit on the floor with Kelly lying flat next to me.

It wasn't long into the prayer time when I got my wish. Jim began to speak in what seemed to be Mary's words. "Look at Kelly. Do you see how happy see is? She is happy because she has Jesus in her heart."

I was the proud mother. Relief mixed with my own happiness within my heart. Mary knew about Kelly. Our prayers were heard. I stroked my daughter's hair, thanking God for giving me what I needed. I'd received a wonderful message. Although I wanted another message, I figured that was the extent, so I reveled in the joy of what I'd received.

But then a few minutes later Jim spoke again. I hadn't expected any other messages, so I was stunned when Jim said, "Bring Kelly to the middle of the room. Everyone gather around her and place your hands on her."

I could barely pick up my daughter, I was shaking so much.

This is it. After everything I've done to make this happen, this is it! I thought. *She's going to be healed!* I was sure of it because everyone had placed their hands on Nancy when she was miscarrying in Medjugorje and she'd been healed. I felt so excited I wanted to cry. I slowly and gently took Kelly to the center of the group and laid her flat on the floor while everyone moved off their chairs and gathered around Kelly as they placed their hands on her.

Within just a few seconds, Jim spoke again. "Do you see the way you look at Kelly with so much love? It is the same way I look at you. You see yourselves as old and worn out, but I see you as young and beautiful. I see you with just as much love as how you look at Kelly.... There are many prayers for Kelly's healing... but you need to pray that God's will is done in her life."

And with those words, the message was over. Silence hung in the air.

As everyone reluctantly rose and slowly returned to their seats, I remained in the center of the room, with my hand still on Kelly's tummy, tears erupting.

What had just happened? Where's the healing? That *wasn't* the message I wanted. And a stunning realization sliced my heart from top to bottom.

Kelly would not be healed.

CHAPTER 18

A Tough Surrender

All hope gone, I spent a sleepless night, tossing and turning, arguing and pleading with God. My prayers felt stifled by my own desires. I wanted God's will—but I wanted God's will to be that Kelly would be healed. I mean, why wouldn't he want to heal her? He had the power. And she was an innocent little life. What reason would there be to take her life? So much more could be accomplished by saving her.

I kept praying, "God, think of the people whose lives would be changed by witnessing that miracle in their midst. Because there would be no denying it! All the medical people would see it, which would be phenomenal! It would change people's lives forever. I can't understand why you wouldn't want that to happen."

But God responded with silence.

I felt as though I would have to shoulder this cross alone. We couldn't squirm or work our way out of it. My daughter was going to die. No explanation or reason, only that God was asking me to trust him, to stay close to him, and to bear this suffering.

And I simply did not want to. It wasn't fair. Period.

Then I thought of Mary. As the mother of Jesus, she never asked to understand, yet she always stood by her son. She never left him alone in his suffering. She trusted that God's will was being done as Christ carried his cross to death. I am sure that she couldn't understand why her son had to die—and die such a horrible death. But Mary never interfered. She never raged against the religious leaders or beat upon the Romans who led him to his execution. She stood by his side every moment and supported him until the end. She trusted there was some meaning to it all.

As dawn wiggled its light around the edges of the bedroom shades, I finally prayed the only thing I had left to say. "God, give me the strength and trust of Mary. Help me to stand by Kelly. Reinforce my faith during the difficult times that are on the horizon. I know I will have to watch my beautiful, innocent baby girl suffer and struggle to breathe until one moment she will no longer be able to continue, and she will die."

And I would be left holding my child, as Mary held her son, pierced through with pain. Trusting there was some meaning to all of it.

I finally arose to greet a somber morning. The car was quiet as we headed to the airport. Jim drove us and stayed with me as I stood in line to get my boarding passes. Oddly enough, I was able only to get my boarding pass for the first flight. The ticket for my connecting flight was, for some reason, rejected. I was concerned because I didn't want to be stranded somewhere with Kelly and unable to get home or help if she needed it. The attendant called a supervisor, who was also unable to issue me the boarding pass, but assured me I would receive one at the connecting flight in Seattle. Jim and I hugged goodbye and he blessed little Kelly once again.

The first leg of our flight went smoothly. I landed and headed to the gate of my connecting flight only to find the same problem: my boarding pass could not be issued. This time, two supervisors were unable to correct the problem, but I was assured I would be able to get on the flight, even if they had to handwrite a boarding pass. They told me to return to the gate at boarding time and I would receive it.

For an hour I walked around the airport keeping Kelly busy until it was time to board. I was weary from the lack of sleep and the weight I carried within my heart. I returned to the gate at boarding time and, as promised, I obtained a boarding pass.

I had been given an aisle seat and prayed that the middle seat beside me would stay empty. That way I could lay Kelly flat upon it and she would be comfortable. But just as I finished that thought, I looked up to see a young man in his early twenties, dressed in military camouflage, staring back at me. Having spent nine years in the Navy, I instantly recognized him to be a Navy SEAL. He motioned that he had the middle seat.

Of course, I thought, *that's what I get for being selfish and wanting it for myself.*

He wiggled past us and settled into his seat, and I noticed that he looked as if his mind were a million miles away. I didn't want to spend the entire flight next to him in an awkward way, especially since we clearly had something in common, so once the airplane lifted off the runway, I mentioned to him that I had been a Navy flight surgeon and that I had taken care of Navy SEALs and truly admired what it took to become one of this elite military group.

As I was telling him how much I admired his dedication and service, I experienced the same thing as I had with the young medical student in the hospital weeks before. A voice whispered into my soul, *I placed him right beside you. Are you going to deny me?*

Instantly I realized why I had so much trouble receiving my boarding pass. It was so that I would be here, sitting next to this man. We were meant to sit by each other because God wanted me to do something for him.

Inwardly I answered, *I will not deny you, God. What do you want me to do?*

A period of silence followed, until I heard, *I need you to give him something.*

What?

More silence and then, *Your crucifix.*

I had worn a silver crucifix around my neck every day since my first trip to Medjugorje, where I had bought it at a tiny shop on the path leading up to Apparition Hill. Though it was special to me, I had learned my lesson. I would not place a material item before a man's soul. If God wanted me to give my crucifix to him, I would, no matter what it meant to me.

I slowly took off my necklace and removed the crucifix. Then I panicked and shoved it into my jeans pocket.

How in the world was I supposed to give it to him? Just say, "Hey, God wants you to have this"? I could imagine him looking at me as if I were a complete and utter nutcase, ringing the call button, and asking the flight attendant to seat him somewhere else. Frankly, I would not have blamed him.

Finally, I decided the perfect time to give him the crucifix would be once the plane had landed in San Diego. While everyone was grabbing their luggage and waiting for the plane doors to open, I could give hand it to him and we would go our separate ways.

Yes, that was a good plan. It seemed doable and not too embarrassing. I just began to settle back in my seat for the rest of the flight when a feeling of intense anxiety came over me. I realized that if I didn't give that crucifix to him now, I would have no peace for the rest of the flight.

Resigned to my mission, I took the crucifix out of my pocket and looked at it, wondering how I should go about handing it over when he suddenly looked at me.

"Do you believe in chance or do you believe in fate?" I asked him.

He simply looked at me and answered nonchalantly, "I believe in chance."

"I used to, but now I don't believe anything happens by chance. I know we were supposed to sit next to each other." I took a deep breath, and before I could give it a second thought, I said, "You're going to think I am crazy, and that's okay. But sometimes I get these messages and I just got one now. I'm supposed to give you something, and I would like to give it to you now if that's okay."

I paused to see how he would respond.

"Okay," he said, acting as if it were no big deal.

This is too easy, I thought. I placed the crucifix in his hand. "I'm supposed to give you this."

He looked at it, then at me. "Well, that is kind of crazy."

My heart fell. "I know," I said, laughing nervously. I didn't know what to say or do, when suddenly I *heard myself say*, "And I'm supposed to tell you something."

Where did that come from? I thought in a panic. My heart began to race and I felt sick. I started to struggle inwardly with God. *Tell him something? God, you never said that! You said, "Give him something." I gave him something and I am done. Now what am I supposed to say? I have no idea!*

The man was looking expectantly at me. I started to move my mouth, hoping something sensible would come out, when I heard myself tell him, "I am supposed to tell you that he loves you very much and that he *does* hear you."

I was still trying to understand what had just happened when I saw his eyes fill with tears as he dropped his face into his hands. He gave a full body sigh and then looked back up at me.

"You have no idea what that means to me. Thank you for telling me that."

All I could get out was, "You know that isn't from me."

"No, I know it's not from you. It couldn't be from you. But thank you for telling me. Thank you."

"Whatever it is, God doesn't do things to hurt us. It's all for our good. We just don't understand. But he loves us so much. We all have crosses, and for some reason we're asked to carry those crosses." I looked down at Kelly. "This little one is going to die. And I don't understand why God is allowing it, but I know that I have to trust him with that, that he sees the bigger picture. That's my cross. And I know if we turn our crosses over to God, somehow that draws us closer to him."

He nodded his understanding and then closed his eyes to pray. For almost two hours, he held the crucifix in his hands. Every once in a while he would look at it, then close his hands around it again, holding it close to his chest in prayer. I suddenly realized I couldn't have given him that crucifix at the end of the flight; he needed time to pray and deal with whatever was going on inside him right then and there.

As we were leaving the plane, he said again, "I really want to thank you for giving me that message. You don't know what it means to me."

"You're welcome." I had done nothing special except be obedient. But God had allowed me to minister to this hurting man. Seeing the difference my obedience made to that SEAL made me realize how important it is to follow God's leading—even when I don't understand why. Everyone's heart is waiting and hoping to be touched by God. I felt privileged to have been such an intermediary for God and realized how much he depends upon us to comfort those around us.

It felt amazing to be able to comfort somebody for God. I had shown God's love to somebody. My whole body tingled with excitement. I was so grateful he'd given me another chance to respond to his call.

Now I had to figure out how I could feel so elated about helping this man when my life circumstances hadn't changed. My daughter was still going to die. And I knew that I needed to heed the words that I'd given to the Navy SEAL.

When I arrived home, Drew immediately wanted to know how it had gone. I could see the light of hope in his eyes. I had once carried that same look of anticipation.

"Did Wayne pray over Kelly?"

"Yes, but..." I paused, wanting to spare Drew the pain of the message I'd received.

"But...?" he pressed on.

I explained about Jim getting messages when he prays the rosary.

"Are you kidding me?" His eyes now turned skeptical. "This is a little much."

"I know, Drew, but I believe him. I do. I know it's hard, I understand that."

"Okay, so did you get a message about Kelly?"

I nodded. "The message wasn't good. It doesn't appear to be God's will that Kelly live."

Agony crossed his face as he tried to grasp what I was saying. My heart ached to watch him. I wanted to spare him the pain of this situation.

"Well, I'm not so sure about this whole thing, you know?" he said. "That message isn't necessarily the final word. We'll just see what God has in mind for Kelly. We'll just see. We're going to continue to pray."

"Absolutely! Of course we'll continue to pray." And we did. Every night we asked God for healing, but my heart wasn't so hopeful. I'd lost my frantic drive. I felt as though the proverbial carpet had been pulled out from under my feet. And I couldn't help but think, *Well, it's done. It's over.*

After all I'd gone through and worked for, I got nothing. Nothing changed. I'd given it everything I had and I'd lost. Now all I could do was stop fighting and leave everything in God's hands, trusting that he really did know what he was doing.

It was the most difficult surrender of my life.

CHAPTER 19

Another Child?

The days passed and I continued to care for my child, determined to give her the best of what life she had left. One evening I gave her a warm bath and then fed her slowly, being careful not to choke her on her formula. As I put her down to bed that night, I kissed her on the forehead and smiled at her. She was beautiful.

This whole time I'd argued with God and pleaded for a miracle and when I didn't get my way, I felt as though I'd been cheated. That I'd done all those religious things for nothing. But now, looking into the smiling face of this precious girl, I knew that it hadn't all been for nothing. If the choice had been not to have Kelly or have Kelly for only this brief time on earth, I would do every bit of it again. This child had touched my heart in a way no one else could.

I had always believed that my child was broken, so I had to find someone and some way to fix her, to make her whole. But that wasn't true at all. My child was not broken. She did not need to be fixed. She was perfect in every way. She was exactly the way God wanted her to be.

All life is good, and all life has meaning. It doesn't matter what stage or what condition it is in. Different lives bring different graces to us. We look for and expect to find God in the "whole," but truly, God is hiding in the "broken."

As I held her little fingers, laying limp at her sides, I wondered who it is who truly has special needs. Those like Kelly who radiate nothing but peace and love, or the physically "perfect"? I saw that when we exclude people like Kelly from our lives, we only limit our own growth. Yes, they bring pain, but when have we ever grown without pain or struggle?

As I watched Kelly drift off to sleep, I began to think about what gives life value. My grandfather lived until he was only a few months shy of one hundred years. Did that mean that his life had more value than Kelly's, who had just months to live? I was raised to believe a life had to be productive to have value, but Kelly was so weak she couldn't physically produce anything. In God's quiet goodness and mercy, he showed me that the value of a life is not based on how much a person produces or even how long he or she lives. The value of life is based simply on how much love it brings forth.

Kelly brought forth unfathomable love. She transformed my husband, my children, our extended family, and me. Because of her, we now had a love and a peace in our lives that never would have existed without her. She brought forth love among my friends as well. They began to pray with their families and viewed their children as precious gifts, not knowing how much time they had together.

I loved this little girl immensely.

I silently turned on her monitor and closed the door behind me. In the kitchen, I stopped to shuffle through that day's mail. The most recent copy of *Medjugorje* magazine had arrived, which I'd subscribed to after my first visit there. I began to leaf through the pages and stopped on a photo of a priest with a wound in the shape of a cross on his forehead. As I scanned the article, I read that this priest, Father Sudac, from Croatia, had suddenly and supernaturally received the wound in May 1999. The following year he received crucifixion wounds, the same type of wounds Christ sustained at his crucifixion. All the wounds had been extensively examined by doctors at the Vatican, who determined that they were not self-inflicted but that he'd received them mystically. Clearly this was a holy man, I thought.

As I read on, Father Sudac had asked the question: "When you die and go to heaven, and Christ is looking deep into your eyes and asks you, 'Who are you?' what are you going to say?"

The question stayed with me and I began to ponder and pray over it. Though I had never imagined myself in that situation before, I knew it would happen one day. One day I will die and stand before the Lord, and how will I summarize my life? Who am I to Christ?

Initially I came up with answers such as my name and profession. But I quickly knew this was senseless; Jesus already knew my name. And my profession is what I do, it is not who I am. It doesn't define me.

And then I came up with another answer: I am a wife and a mother. Of all the answers I had thought of, I knew this was the best. Christ values marriage and motherhood very highly. At the same time, although I knew that answer would have sufficed, I thought it lacked in some way. I wanted my relationship with Christ to be more. I wanted it to be special. More special than any earthly relationship.

I suddenly realized that he wanted to know if I had a personal relationship with him. Did I pray to him? Did he know me? I could answer yes, but it still wasn't enough. I wanted *more*.

I loved Christ so much I not only wanted him to know me fully, I wanted to serve him, to bring others to him so that they too can experience a personal relationship with him.

I knew what I truly want to say to him when he asks me, "Who are you?" I want to say: "I am a child of God, and I am the servant of your love. I have spent my life doing things for you because I love you. *Only* because I love you." That is what I want to say. And I would never have come to that realization without Kelly.

As I began to look at Kelly differently—not as a broken child, but as a true gift just the way she was—I became more willing to discuss the possibility of having another child. Drew had always wanted a large family and after having four kids, another one didn't seem to be out of the question. But the lingering anxiety came: what if our next child had the same issue as Kelly? Could I go through this experience again? The pain of what we were enduring made for an easy answer: no.

But rather than shutting down the possibility, Drew and I began to wonder if God was asking us to have more children. We wanted to be obedient to him. And really, I couldn't imagine that he would ask us to go through the same thing with another child.

We were at a crossroads. I was trying to follow every guideline and precept of the Catholic Church. I believe that the church cares deeply for the safety of everyone's soul and their life in this world. If the church says no to artificial contraception, then I would follow that. But at the same time, I was carrying a genetic disorder. God gave us our intellect and expects us to use it to make good, thoughtful decisions.

What is the responsible thing to do? I wondered. *Should I risk having more children with this disorder? Is that responsible?*

Drew and I continued to wonder and pray and finally we decided to visit our priest for spiritual guidance. After listening to our situation, he looked at us sincerely and said that the church would never tell us *not* to have any more children if we desired it, but it would not ask it of us either.

"Whatever you decide," he told us, "the church will support."

I left the meeting unsettled. We still didn't have an answer. What should we do? Both Drew and I wanted more children, and yet there was the risk.

We continued to struggle over what to do. If God wanted me to have more children, I would—even if it meant having another child with SMA. I just *didn't know* what God wanted. And even as I prayed about it, I received no clear indication either way.

About a week after our visit with the priest, as I was looking through our mail I discovered a letter addressed to me from Jim. I opened the envelope to find a short note and a yellow card with handwriting on the front and back.

The letter read:

Dear Cyndi,

Our Lady came and gave this message for you at 3 a.m. on 5-22-02. Hope it all means something to you. Only you and her [sic] know what your heart needs to know.

With my hands trembling, I looked at the yellow card in my other hand. I had received a message from Mary? As I read, my knees almost gave way by the words.

My daughter,
Don't let your womb grow cold.
   Kelly is a gift that is your and my hearts combined with God's love.
   My daughter, keep focused on Jesus and our love for you and your family. Don't be afraid. I am with you, my child. My mantle of protection is covering you and your family. Keep placing our hearts together. They will become one in total love of Jesus. Feel the people in our hearts combined with my Son's. Nothing is impossible, my daughter.
   Pray, pray, pray.
Love,
Mom

I loved that she signed it Mom! Here was my answer: *Don't let your womb grow cold.* We were to have more children. My prayers had been answered in a way I never could have imagined.
   I immediately went to find Drew. He was working out in our garage that we had converted into a basic gym. My heart racing,

I forced myself to calm down and approach him as casually as possible.

"Hey, Drew. I just got a letter from Mary. Do you want to hear it?"

It took him a moment to realize I was talking about the Blessed Mother, but as soon as it connected he stopped abruptly. "Yes!"

I read the letter to him and then waited a moment for him to process everything. Finally, I couldn't hold it in any longer. "What do you think?"

"I think we should have another baby." Drew said with a slight smile and a gleam in his eyes. I knew I could not have given him better news.

"Are you sure? You know this could happen again." Even though I knew Drew wanted to have as many children as possible, I needed Drew to understand the depth of what we were possibly being asked to do.

"Cyndi," he said, his eyes pierced with seriousness. "We are being asked to have another child. I am sure."

So we had our answer. As I thought back to the other times when God had asked me to do things I didn't understand—such as talking with the Navy SEAL—I realized that sometimes God does ask us to do things that seem crazy, but he is faithful and always has a reason for our good. So as difficult as it was to accept—because of the fear that this next child could also receive the same diagnosis—I decided to trust the message. Now it was time to see where that trust would take us.

The real surprise came when I learned how strong some people's opinions were about our decision. Not long after we'd decided to allow ourselves to have another child, I visited the ob-gyn with Kelly for a post-pregnancy checkup.

"Okay, so what kind of birth control do you want to use?" she asked.

"I'm not going to use any."

The woman put down her pen and looked sternly at me. "What did you say?"

"I'm not going to use any birth control."

She inhaled sharply. "Is this for your religion?"

"Yes, absolutely."

"You're going to end up just like my mother. You're going to end up pregnant. You're going to have to stop working altogether, and everything's going to be lost. Okay. All right. Well, good luck."

I never went back to her! No matter what decision I made, no one had the right—even my physician—to belittle me and my choice. And what was it to her anyway? What was it to her if I did completely stop practicing medicine and choose to raise my family? Was that the worst thing in the world?

I understood that not everyone would grasp our decision. I understood that not everyone would be able to sign up for the possibility of having another child. But I also understood that when God calls us to do something—whether or not it makes sense to our human minds—we need to obey. I wasn't excited about possibly signing up for more heartache. But I was committed to signing up for whatever God called me to do. How could I possibly do otherwise?

CHAPTER 20

The Deepest Pain

Soon Kelly's health worsened again and she was admitted to the ICU one more time with the same diagnosis. This time, she was so weak that she was unable to fight back, despite the aggressive treatment she was given.

Finally, after she had been in the hospital for seventeen days, the doctors approached us.

"There's nothing more we can do for Kelly," one doctor informed Drew and me. "You can leave Kelly here and we'll care for her until she dies, or you can take her home and she can die there."

We needed no discussion. We knew she needed to be home. Drew removed the tubes and wires from Kelly while I handled the paperwork. Twenty minutes later, we were headed home with our baby. She struggled just to breathe and I worried that she would die on the way. I kept praying over her, as Drew sped up and swerved through traffic to get home as quickly as we could. Miraculously, once at home, Kelly seemed to rebound and began to regain her strength. Having her brothers around her seemed to pick up her spirits, and her eyes were filled with joy once again.

We called hospice to set up care for Kelly. They were wonderfully sensitive and helpful. They provided all the same equipment that she had in the ICU, including a nasogastric tube running from her nose into her stomach to feed her, oxygen, as well as a device that would inflate her lungs as she took in a breath, a suctioning machine, an oxygen monitor, pain medicine, and antibiotics. The care was exhausting and constant, but there was nothing I would rather do. Each day with my baby was precious because we never knew if it would be our last.

One bright September morning, six weeks later, I went into Kelly's bedroom to check on her. I took one look at her and knew she had only minutes left. Her breathing was very slow with long stretches between each breath. Her eyes were slightly glazed over.

I yelled for Drew and the boys to come quickly and then I picked her up and gently caressed her. Before I had always tried to hold my tears back, but this time I let them stream freely down my face and onto her little body.

Drew and the boys ran into the room looking scared. As soon as Drew saw me, he tenderly removed all the tubes and wires from Kelly. Then I slowly dropped to my knees, gently holding Kelly in my arms so everyone could place their hands on her one last time. Sobs escaped my lips as I tried to stop time. Just a few more minutes. Just a little more time, I begged God. We all knelt around her and she took her last breath.

She was gone and my heart ripped in two.

I pulled her into my chest and rocked back and forth.

"God, please take me too. I don't want to live anymore, it's too hard. *Please*." Other sobs filled the room and I opened my eyes to see my husband and my three beautiful boys kneeling, broken and praying.

We bonded in Kelly's life and now our pain and grief bonded us more deeply. I could see that my prayer was birthed out of my agony. I would mourn my daughter, but I had to go on. I had my sons who needed me to be their mom too.

I held Kelly close to me, a small comfort that I was finally able to hold her and not worry about hurting her or making her uncomfortable.

We stayed together in Kelly's room for almost an hour, and then not knowing what else to do, we called the funeral home. We had arranged for Kelly's funeral weeks before. I'd hoped they would take their time arriving, but in what seemed like minutes, they were at the door. Lovingly, we carried Kelly out to the car and she was gone.

I stood outside long after the car left.

Why didn't we wait longer to call? I thought. I had no idea she would be taken away so quickly. I wanted to hold her one more time. I wanted to have another chance to say goodbye.

Finally as in a daze, I slowly made my way back to her room. Her presence was gone. The room felt empty. I grazed my hand over the crib and thought again about all the wonderful years of life she would never experience. I felt dead inside.

The doctors had given Kelly nine months to live. And she died at nine months.

CHAPTER 21

The Funeral

On the day of Kelly's funeral, we had a visitation that morning at the house for the family and close friends. My heart ached and the depression medication I'd been on was no longer working. I sunk into a deep depression and was grateful I was able to take a shower and make myself half presentable. I looked outside at the sunny Southern California weather—so beautiful and perfect. So unlike my spirits. If I could just put one foot in front of the other, I could make it through the day. Everything felt like a haze. I couldn't quite connect what was happening, as though my perception of everything was delayed, and I felt as if all I could do was go through the motions. I wanted this day to end—but really, I'd wanted this day never to have come.

Because Kelly had been so small, the morticians had to make a little casket for her. They brought the casket in and set it on a small decorative chest of drawers in the entryway. From there they took Kelly and laid her in her crib with her blankets and stuffed animals. We would have several hours to be with her before everything moved to St. James's church for the funeral. Kelly looked beautiful and so tiny. She was truly at peace.

Soon the house filled with people wanting to pay their final respects and to offer comfort. A neighbor and close friend, Virginia Langdon, arrived early and presented me with a handmade crown of pink baby roses to place on Kelly's head. Before I'd had Kelly, I'd never really known this woman, but when Kelly was diagnosed, she showed up and became a great support. Having lost a child of her own, she understood much of the anguish I was suffering.

I looked over at my boys. I'd dressed them all in little white shirts and matching khaki pants and belts. They looked sad, but seemed to be doing okay. So young to have to take on the weight of the world.

Too soon it was time to leave. As the funeral director and his helper came to move the casket, they accidentally gouged a piece out of the dresser. They apologized but it was the first moment that day I was able to genuinely smile. This was my Kelly mark.

"It's okay," I reassured them. "I like it this way."

The church at St. James was packed. I had never seen so many people show up for a funeral—from schoolchildren and their families to teachers and friends and our own extended family.

To see Drew walk down the center aisle at the beginning of the funeral as he carried his daughter in that little coffin was the saddest sight I had ever seen. The service started soon after, and the priest led some prayers and said a few words about eternal life and Christ's suffering opening the path for us to be able to join him in heaven. I knew his words were meant to bring comfort and support, but my heart was so heavy, I could only listen without really hearing.

Next Rob, Drew's brother and Kelly's godfather, stood and gave a reading. Then our eldest son, Drew Jr., who was eight years old, gave the second reading from 2 Corinthians 4:6-10, which speaks of how the afflictions in this world produce an eternal glory beyond comprehension and how we look not to what is seen and transitory but to what is unseen and eternal. Drew Jr. had wanted to do something special for Kelly, and he did a wonderful job.

Knowing our faith had been so inspired and strengthened by Kelly's life, our pastor had asked us to say a few words to the congregation. Drew spoke first. He told the crowd how much his little daughter had meant to him and how much she had brought our family together. He would never forget the love she shared with us.

Then it was my turn to speak. I'd never wanted to speak in front of people—and certainly never about my faith. Now here I was, standing in front of everyone I knew, ready to speak about Kelly and the God I trust even when I don't understand. I approached the microphone shaking. I had written some words the night before. I was emotionally exhausted and I found myself on the verge of tears. I wasn't sure I would get through it. But this was the last time I would be with my daughter, the last time I would see her, and I wanted to make it special. I wanted to celebrate the joy she had brought into the world and how meaningful her life had been. I prayed to be able to get through this moment.

"Kelly was a gift," I began with a voice that shook. "A gift from God. She would look at you with those eyes full of love and it seemed as if she were looking directly and deeply into your soul. And that smile. Kelly spread such joy and peace in my life, in my family, and in this community. Isn't that what Christ desires of all of us? Aren't we all asked to bring peace and joy to all we meet? Kelly's life truly reflected God's love for us all."

As I continued to speak, my body and voice calmed and I knew this was part of Kelly's ministry. This was *her* message. And if I didn't do it, then Kelly's life would have lost its meaning. That realization gave me strength to know that this was what it was about. And I had to get through it, and I had to do it in a way that wasn't depressing.

"Kelly has forever changed my life. She strengthened my faith, and made me want to become a better person. I believe Kelly was sent as a message to us all. The same message that Mary gave in her first apparition in Medjugorje, when she said, 'I come to tell you that God exists and that he loves you very much.'

"Kelly was able to touch so many people and she truly changed them. For someone who was so weak, who could barely raise her own hand, look at what her inner strength has accomplished in her short life. She kindled love in people's hearts—Christ's love.

"She inspired so many people to pray. I can't thank you enough for all your support and love. It is truly overwhelming. I don't pretend to know God's will, but I do ask that it be done in my life, because I trust he loves us and knows what is best. He sent Kelly to us, not to bring us pain, but to bring us closer to him.

"One person wrote me a letter going over all the 'miracles' Kelly brought to her family. She thought it was meaningful that Kelly had died at nine months of age—the same amount of time it takes to create life. Kelly created life and love in all of us here.

"Her mission is finished and God has called her home. She showed us the importance of prayer and increased our faith in God. I hope to keep what Kelly created alive in our hearts and in our families. I hope we all continue to pray daily and, most importantly, as a family. The only important job we have as parents is to get our children to heaven.

"I have rosaries from our trip with Kelly to Medjugorje. Please take one as a remembrance of Kelly and her message of family prayer.

"Thank you for your prayers for Kelly and our family. Thank you, Kelly, I love you and miss you."

I sat next to Drew and felt that I'd finally gotten the answer to my "why" question. The words I'd just spoken was the message of Kelly's life and it needed to be delivered and it needed to be heard and acted on. The message was to pray. Commit to pray in and for our families. We don't know how long we have with our children, and they need to be formed.

Drew took my hand and we joined with the congregation as the priest prayed the concluding prayers over Kelly. Then the funeral was over. Drew went and again picked up the little coffin, turned, and walked up the aisle with Drew Jr., John, Jack, and me following. Outside, a long, white hearse was waiting with its back door open. Drew placed the coffin inside and stepped back as the funeral director closed the door.

Drew and I held each other as we watched the car drive away.

Soon people were gathering around us, expressing their sorrow and thanking us for the strength of our faith. I handed out three hundred rosaries and when we ran out, I grabbed medals, showing Mary holding baby Jesus in her arms, which I had also brought with me from Medjugorje. Each medal had been present during an apparition in Medjugorje and Mary had blessed them there. The hundred that I had were also all taken. I really wanted people to have something to remember Kelly and remember what her life stood for and what she had done in her brief time here on earth.

One woman approached me in tears. "Oh, Cyndi, you don't understand why I am crying. I listened to you speak and say how we must get our children to heaven. I have had five children and I'm not sure one of them will get there. You are blessed to know that Kelly is there."

I was struck by her words. It was true. I did know Kelly was in heaven. Our priest had baptized and confirmed her several months before she'd died. The knowledge that I would again see my child someday in heaven gave me great comfort. But it didn't make me miss her any less. Many times people think that because we're guaranteed an eternal life because of what Jesus did for us on the cross, that means that somehow we should grieve our losses here on earth less. I didn't find that to be true. Pain is still pain.

After the funeral we went to the parish hall for a reception. Drew and I made our way around talking to people and thanking them for coming as they poured out their heartfelt condolences to us. And then we went home.

And the emptiness heaved itself upon me in relentless waves.

I was so desperately empty and pained. Drew and I walked into Kelly's room and it stood stark, vacant, hollow. Hospice had come during the funeral and removed all the hospital equipment. Kelly really was gone.

I placed my hand on my womb. I had given life, and death had stolen my daughter. How could I even possibly have considered going through this agony again with another child?

I was four months' pregnant.

PART 4
Sarah

CHAPTER 22

"We Can Help You"

The loss we experienced after Kelly's death was immense. I felt as if my heart would never heal.

It took all my energy just to drag myself out of bed every morning. I did because I knew my three boys needed a mother, but I couldn't give them my full attention and nurture. It wasn't that I didn't want to; I was simply unable. I could still muster enough energy to take them to their activities and listen to their days—but in the back of my mind, I had to force myself to be present for them.

Drew was also devastated. His dreams for this child were gone. At least he had his work to go to every day that kept him going. I had quit my job. So my days stretched out before me—barren and threatening to take me over the edge of insanity. I spent as much time as I could with the boys, my prayer group, and at church— seeking solace in the arms of my Father. It was humbling to learn that I had nothing to depend on except God. And I had to cling to him, my only rescuer, and seek him for the small purpose in each day, even if it involved suffering and sacrifice.

I'd spent so much of my life reveling in my independence and ability to solve and handle anything, but I couldn't solve this, and I couldn't make the pain go away on my own. My pride had broken and I was humbled; I couldn't rely on myself anymore for anything.

The one bright spot was that we were having another child. But the weight upon us with the realization that this situation could very well happen again was tremendous and stress became my daily companion. It was an unspoken fear between us. Drew and I never talked openly about the possibility of another diagnosis, but we didn't need to. We believed deeply that God wanted us to have this child, and so we would. But of course, we prayed that this next baby—boy or girl—would be a healthy child to treasure and hold forever. We still carried the love we had for Kelly within us. I'm not sure anyone who has lost a child ever loses that love. A new baby would give us a place to pour that immense love that we didn't know what to do with.

I could sense that people were shocked that I was having another child, given the genetic condition Drew and I carried. After people gained their composure at the news, they quickly encouraged me that the chances of having another child with this disorder were so slim that I shouldn't worry—after all, they told me, "God wouldn't do this to you again. You've already suffered enough." They reminded me that I'd spoken about my faith because of Kelly and that I'd done an awesome job representing Christ to others. That because of Kelly, many people were brought to a saving knowledge of God, so God was sure to reward me with a healthy child.

I wasn't so sure, however. While my pregnancy progressed normally, I couldn't help but be anxious about this child's health. God's ways are not always our ways. I felt certain that God had wanted me to have this child—the only reason I became pregnant in the first place—but for what reason? I braced myself for the possibility that I could indeed have another baby with spinal muscular atrophy (SMA). I prayed that God didn't think I was strong enough to go through all this again, and that he would give me a "normal" child to love. After all, he'd witnessed my deep depression. But I also prayed that if he gave me another child with SMA, he would stand by me with the strength I needed while helping me understand why.

My heart's desire was that I do the will of God. And I did trust he could get me through anything. Of course I wanted the easy and exciting way. Don't we all? But the longer into the pregnancy I went, the more resolved I was that this child would also suffer from SMA. And I would think, *If this baby has SMA, that's going to be really hard to explain to people about God's love.* I thought that I wouldn't put it past the Lord to do this to me again. After all, I had told him that even if the child had SMA, I would have another baby for him. So I couldn't blame him. I understood that certain people do suffer for God. And if that was to be my role and my children's role, whatever part it plays in the bigger plan, then that would be okay, because it's the big picture that counts. I knew that in the end we would be fine anyway.

But I'm human. And it was easy to say that we'd be fine—and even to believe it—but still I hoped with all my heart that God wouldn't ask me to struggle through another round of intense suffering. So even though I knew deep down this next child would suffer from SMA, somehow I talked myself into believing what my friends had said. I became hopeful as I thought, *Yeah, why wouldn't this baby be normal? I'm just making too much out of something that probably isn't going to happen anyway.*

So I was a mixed bag. I wanted desperately to have a normal child. Desperately.

Apparently so did my physician.

Although my pregnancy was easy and uneventful, my obstetrician followed me closely, looking for any evidence that this new baby might be affected in the same way as Kelly. When it came time to check the fetal alpha-protein level to screen for fetal abnormalities, when I was eighteen weeks along, while I knew SMA would never show up on it, I agreed. It was a simple blood test and posed no risk to the baby. If anything else showed up, at least I could be prepared.

At my follow-up visit, the doctor told me the test had come back normal. Then he routinely stated it was time to have an amniocentesis—a medical procedure in which the doctor inserts a needle into the woman's uterus to draw amniotic fluid and test for other abnormalities. I know I startled him when I told him no.

"What do you mean?" He looked perplexed.

"I don't want to do the test." I replied resolutely.

I had never had an "amnio" with any of my four previous pregnancies; I didn't see the need for it. I knew that I would never abort a child, and no information I could be given could possibly change my mind. Unlike the previous blood test, this one did carry a risk: there was a roughly 1 percent risk of miscarriage. It didn't matter how small the percentage, I was unwilling to take it. Moreover, I had remembered a case in medical school in which a needle had mistakenly entered the eye of a fetus during an amniocentesis. The baby was born blind in that eye. If I wasn't going to use the information, why put my child at any risk?

Undeterred, he pressed again. "You know, with your history, it might make a lot of sense."

"You're probably right, but I really don't want to put the baby at risk. Besides, no matter what, I am going to have the child. Even if it does have SMA."

At that point, he suggested a comprehensive ultrasound, to which I easily agreed. I would be able to see my baby, but I seriously doubted anything could be gained from it.

At twenty-one weeks, the time came for my ultrasound, and I was excited to see this baby. I could feel it moving and wondered what it looked like. I still didn't know if it was a boy or girl, and I didn't want the technician to tell me. Drew and I were keeping it a surprise.

The technician performed the in-depth examination and showed me several images of my child. He asked me questions about Kelly and my pregnancy with her, and then left to show the images to the physician on duty.

He was gone for what seemed like hours. I knew they were discussing how this child could potentially have SMA. They had to be sure, and they needed to look for any signs of the disorder that might be evident on an ultrasound. I knew they wouldn't be able to find anything, but the wait made me think that perhaps they *had* seen something. Maybe it was something else entirely, something I hadn't even considered.

Maybe the baby has Down syndrome, I thought.

Finally the doctor, a well-dressed, fit, Middle Eastern man in his early thirties, entered the room. He introduced himself and then went on to perform the same ultrasound evaluation the technician had just done. Without giving me any information, he asked me to dress and meet him in his office, and he left.

Now I was on edge.

I entered his office and found a brightly lit, immaculately clean room lined with books and smelling of coffee. Framed diplomas and certificates of completion covered the majority of the far wall of his office. A single framed photo of his three smiling children sat on the desk he now sat behind. He motioned to a chair opposite his desk and I sat. The doctor asked me questions about Kelly, her diagnosis, my pregnancy with her, and what her symptoms had been. Before long, it became clear that I knew much more about SMA than he did.

Then the conversation took a new turn.

"Your ultrasound is completely normal. And I want you to know I distinctly saw the fetus move," he said.

Relieved there was no evidence of Down syndrome, I started to relax. It was nice that he wanted me to know the baby had moved, but I had to laugh. I mean, I could feel the baby move. No one had to tell me.

I thanked him and began to get up.

"Wait."

I paused.

"You need to know that we can help you."

I sat back down and looked him directly in the eyes. "What do you mean?"

"You need to know that we can tell you if this baby has SMA."

I knew the procedure he was referring to. "Thank you, but I am going to have this baby." *That should put the issue to rest,* I thought. I was mistaken.

"But we can help you. You don't have to go through all of that pain. You need to know we can help you." He leaned forward in his chair and looked directly at me.

I could tell he didn't truly believe anyone would continue a pregnancy if the baby had SMA. This time I answered more firmly. "Thank you. I appreciate that, I really do. But I *am going to have this baby*." I shifted in my chair. I knew he was just trying to help me in his own way, but I wanted no part of it. Unfortunately, he was relentless.

"You need to know that we have the means of diagnosing if this pregnancy is positive for SMA. Then you will have the information." He continued to look intently at me, never taking his eyes from me.

"The information for what?"

"So you can decide what to do." His voice was cool and professional.

By now, I was getting angry. I could feel the blood color my face. I had already told him twice I was going to have this baby. What was it that he didn't understand? When I looked at him next, I saw the compassion in his eyes; he truly wanted to save me from any pain he could.

But I also saw something else very clearly: if I hadn't been firm in my decision before coming to this office about my decision never to have an abortion, regardless of the circumstances, it would have been easy to be talked into having an amnio.

"Exactly how would you get that information?" I decided to ask. What if there was something that could be done that didn't put the baby at risk? I could at least hear him out.

"At this stage in the fetus's development, we would have to take a sample of its blood. That sample would be analyzed and you would have the ability to decide."

"What are the risks of this procedure?" I was horrified at the thought of a needle not just piercing the fluid surrounding the baby, but the baby itself.

"The risk of a miscarriage is 5 percent, higher than a routine amniocentesis, but this is more invasive. You would, however, be able to make the decision."

He kept repeating about my need to make a decision. His heart was bleeding for me. He truly wanted to help. But his help was by letting me know that if my child had SMA I could abort it and be saved all the emotional anguish associated with having a child who would die. The fact that he wanted to save me the pain was noble, but I would have to end my own child's life in order to do that. What he didn't understand, and what wasn't noble, was that doing so would have totally destroyed me. I would never have been able to live with myself. His answer was an easy way to take a cross out of my life, but in avoiding this suffering, I would endure a new one, and be forever changed. What he failed to appreciate was that we grow only when we suffer, no matter how unbelievably painful it can be. And I trusted God. He wanted this baby, I believed, so I would have this baby no matter what.

"You need to understand something," I said. "I will do nothing to risk this child's life. I am going to have this baby."

His eyebrows knitted together in shock and concern. "You mean to tell me you are going to have this baby, no matter what?"

Had he been listening at all? I was sure he rarely ran across mothers like me.

"No matter what." I looked straight in his eyes.

Silence.

Finally, he spoke in an incredulous tone. "Then I guess we don't need to see you anymore."

I was relieved that he finally understood, and I couldn't wait to get out of there. I wanted to scream.

He leaned back in his chair and spoke slowly. "I know exactly how you feel. I have three children of my own."

I was dumbfounded. How could he possibly know how I felt? To have a child who was going to die and possibly have another one. Did he know what that was like? Did he know the love of that kind of a child?

I smiled, thanked him for his time, and left the office angry with myself for not seeing any of that coming. How naïve was I? I should have realized that this ultrasound was going to be different, that this issue would be raised. But it didn't matter.

I had seen my baby and it looked perfect.

CHAPTER 23

A Healthy Baby Girl!

I prayed continuously throughout my pregnancy that God's will be done in the life of this child. If he were to grace us with a healthy child, I would forever be grateful and thankful. I also prayed that if God asked us to care for another child with special needs, then he give us the strength to do so. Without his support, I would be utterly crushed.

As my delivery date neared, I found myself thinking often about Kelly's birth. She had seemed so much at peace, so relaxed. She never squirmed or cried much. At the time I had thought she was an angel, gentle and perfect. Now I realized that she had been weak from the beginning. Even throughout my pregnancy with her, I barely felt her gentle pushes. I was much more aware of those things with this pregnancy, and was overjoyed to feel strong, prominent kicks. My hopes rose.

As with my previous pregnancies, I was two weeks past my due date, so on February 23, 2003, my physician admitted me to the hospital and placed me again on a Pitocin drip to induce labor. I slowly began to experience contractions that gained in strength and frequency over time. Finally, after hours of this, my doctor told me to start pushing.

Several pediatric specialists were present for my delivery, and the staff of the neonatal intensive care unit was standing by. As I geared up to begin pushing, I couldn't help but feel an intense anxiety grip my heart. What would this child be? Would it have SMA?

On my third push, the obstetrician happily announced it was another girl. I was overjoyed. Of course it was a girl, I thought. What else could she have been? God had graced us with another beautiful baby girl—Sarah Kelly Peterson.

The look on Drew's face when he gazed into our little girl's eyes for the first time was one of pure happiness.

And then came that horrible moment, as everyone began to examine my baby. The flurry of activity only made it worse. Everyone huddled around the incubator, obscuring my view of Sarah. Was there something wrong? What were they doing? My obstetrician began drawing blood samples from the umbilical cord. He explained he would send these for analysis to determine if Sarah had SMA.

I understood his desire. But I had seen this child *move* and heard her cry. That was more than Kelly had ever done, so I was sure she was fine. The fear that had such a strong hold on me even just moments before, now relaxed and eased its way out of my body with each new cry I heard.

Slowly everyone moved away and a nurse handed my baby to me.

"She has excellent Apgar scores," the nurse told me. Again, I breathed in deeply at the news. The Apgar scores offer an initial assessment of how strong and viable an infant is. "And she's breathing normally on her own. We found no defects. Your baby appears to be normal."

"Thank you," I said, unable to remove my eyes from this beautiful little girl. I understood why they were being careful not to declare she *didn't* have SMA, but all appeared to be fine at this point.

Tears of joy began to flow down my cheeks as I held my baby girl. I laughed as she squirmed in my arms. She was normal.

"Thank you, God," I whispered as I placed my lips on Sarah's forehead. I was in disbelief. I had prepared myself for the worst, but it was all for nothing! Sarah Kelly Peterson was strong.

News spread quickly that Sarah had come out kicking. I hadn't realized how much everyone had been on edge until I saw the relief and happiness in their eyes as they stopped by to see and hold my baby.

Although she seemed strong, the doctors kept her in the neonatal intensive care unit for precautionary measures and for continued observation. They even wanted her to stay an additional day, but they observed nothing worrisome. We came home three days after her birth to the delight of three excited little boys, eager to hold their baby sister.

"Will this baby live?" Drew Jr. asked, while his brothers listened in.

"It's up to God, but I think she will. She's strong."

Although Kelly had resembled her brother Drew, Sarah took after her brother John. She had a darker complexion, straight brown hair and deep brown eyes. Where Kelly's features had been fine in nature, Sarah's were more prominent. She had a special inner strength and beauty about her.

My favorite thing to do with Sarah, other than look at her and cuddle with her, was believe it or not, to change her diapers! She kicked so much I'd have to work at pulling down her legs just to put her diaper on. I loved that I had to struggle with her. And every time I did, I thought, *This is so great. She's strong! Thank you, God, thank you! I have a normal child.*

I began to think about the future again and my depression slowly lifted. I still grieved Kelly and the loss of her future, but Sarah now held my dreams. Our family was complete. Perfect.

At Sarah's first visit to the pediatrician, everything checked out fine. Unfortunately, they had nothing in her chart about the blood samples they'd taken right after she was born to check for SMA, but my pediatrician said he would follow up on it and get back to me. I just wanted to confirm that nothing was wrong, and then I could enjoy my baby.

Later that day, I received a phone call informing me that the blood samples sent from the hospital had been contaminated. They could not be used because my blood had been mixed in with Sarah's. Now there was only one way to be sure, and that was to have a blood sample taken from Sarah herself. I almost laughed. I didn't need a blood test to tell me my daughter was normal. She moved all the time! While the medical professionals encouraged me to have Sarah's blood tested to put the issue to rest, and Drew agreed, *I* knew there was nothing to worry about. This child was different. I really didn't want to hurt Sarah with the blood draw, but to appease everyone, I agreed to another blood test. This would finally put the issue to rest. So three days later, I took Sarah to the clinic's laboratory.

"Hi, baby girl," the lab technician said sweetly to Sarah, who didn't seem happy to be poked with a needle and she whined and jostled restlessly about. "So this blood draw is for an SMA test. I've never even heard of that. What is it, if you don't mind my asking?"

I told her briefly about SMA and Kelly.

She stared at me in disbelief and then looked down at Sarah, who was still wiggling around. "But she looks so normal. She's a beautiful little girl."

"That's just it. Everything is normal about SMA kids at first, except they grow weak and eventually can't move. They are normal in every other way. They look just as normal as Sarah here." As I said the words, I felt something inside of me sink. *No, this baby is fine*, I told myself. She was a gift. Sarah was nothing like Kelly; she was strong and perfect. Surely God wouldn't do this to us again.

CHAPTER 24

Blindsided

I quickly forgot about the blood test as our family got on with our lives. The haze that had covered my mind and thoughts for so long with the depression had lifted and I felt more alive and like myself than I had for years. I had more energy and enjoyed my role as wife and mother. Life was good again.

Almost three weeks later, Sarah and I were enjoying a lively game of peek-a-boo and giggling joyfully. We were interrupted by the phone ringing. I knew it was Drew because he would always call during the day to see what we were up to.

"Sarah and I are just lying on the carpet here in the family room, playing peek-a-boo together," I told him in a light tone.

Usually he would have responded with, "Oh, that's so great. I wish I were there." But instead, he paused, then in a matter-of-fact tone, he said, "I have some news about Sarah."

"Oh yeah? Is it that she's a great little girl?"

"Are you alone?"

"Yeah. Well, I've got Sarah here."

"Is that it?"

"Yeah."

"Are you sitting down?"

"I'm lying down. What's up?"

"I just got the results on Sarah's blood test." His voice was in doctor mode. Unemotional. Just forwarding the news.

I laughed. "And they're normal, right?" I reached over and tickled Sarah.

"No, Cyndi. They're not."

His words hit me like a punch. "What do you mean?" I immediately sat up.

"Sarah has the same diagnosis as Kelly."

"No, Drew. No, no, no. How can that be? She is strong! The test is wrong, Drew. It's wrong!"

"Cyndi, the results say she has SMA." He said it softly, in a way that left no room for further denial.

"Oh, my God. Oh, God." I looked again at Sarah. She was wiggling and gurgling and happy. And I knew the test wasn't wrong.

Why? It was all I could think. *What is the point?* The darkness fell like a thud over my heart again. Anger and hurt felt like a fist around my insides and I thought I would throw up. The room began to spin and tears filled my eyes.

"Are you okay?"

I opened my mouth, but all that would come was a whisper. "No, I'm not okay. Are you okay?"

"No."

"I don't want to do this all over again. It's too hard. I *can't* do this all over again." As I said it, I reached out and grabbed a chair, something solid to hold onto, and heaved myself into it, leaving Sarah by me on the floor.

"Cyndi," he said, "we'll get through this. God has some reason for all of this. We have to trust him. It will be okay in the end. We have to trust. We have to."

He was right. "I know. But it's hard."

"I know. I'm not going to pretend I'm not devastated by this, but we have to hang in there."

"Okay."

"I don't want you to be alone. I've already told the news to Martha," he continued. Martha was my best friend, who lived down the street from me. "I want you to go over there. Take Sarah and talk to her. Promise me. I need to know you are with someone."

"Fine." I was angry that he told Martha before he told me, even though I knew he did it only so that I would have somebody to go to. I pressed my eyes closed and sat. I had no intention of going to Martha's. Or anywhere.

"Promise me, Cyndi. Promise you'll go over there."

"I'll be okay, I don't need to go—"

"Promise me."

I gritted my teeth together. "All right, fine. I'll go over there."

He seemed satisfied. "Call me if you need anything. I'll be home early tonight. We'll get through this."

I hung up as the sobs that had held back in my throat erupted.

"Why, God? No one's going to understand this. *No one.* How am I going to tell people? This is crazy! No one will understand. This is going to drive people away from you, you know that, right?" My sobs turned angry. "Well, you know what? I'm not taking her anywhere. If this is the baby who's going to be healed and this is the big miracle, you can do it right here, because I'm not going to ask for it, and I'm not going to take her to anybody and I'm not taking her to Medjugorje. And if you want to heal her, you can do it yourself. You're powerful. You can do it on your own right here."

I picked Sarah up and put her in her car seat and drove to Martha's. When Martha opened the door, I walked in, placed Sarah on the couch, still in her car seat, and turned back to look at my friend. I tried to talk, to say something, but nothing would come out. We just hugged each other and cried.

For days I wandered around lost. My joy was replaced by hopelessness. I knew what was ahead of me. I had lived it once before. Sorrow would pierce my heart as it had with Kelly. I knew the fear and the struggles ahead of us both. What could possibly be the reason for such a thing? Why would I be asked to have a child and then have the same diagnosis? Anger and disbelief would rise within me. I didn't understand, but deep inside, somehow, I still trusted. I just really needed to know that this was truly God's will. To know that would make the journey ahead of me bearable. This couldn't just be some random statistic. This couldn't be just chance. And deep inside I still desperately wanted a miracle. But I was afraid to let my hope rise, to let myself become so vulnerable again only to be crushed.

I'd called our priest to have Sarah baptized and confirmed, so at least that weight was off my mind. And I didn't want to try to fight the diagnosis. I wasn't okay with it, but I'd accepted that it was what it was. I knew that, in the end, Sarah would be in heaven, and as a mother that gave me comfort. But I still struggled with why this had to happen and whether it really was God's will for Sarah and our family to suffer this way.

I went back on prescription medication for the depression, which had returned in full force. And I was dead tired—to the point that while I was driving, I would look for places to pull to the side of the road to nap. That lack of sleep made everything sound hollow and I spent much of my time trying to process things just to keep up with the daily routine.

Many times during Kelly's life I had prayed with her in front of the tabernacle in our church, where Catholics believe Jesus is truly present—body, blood, soul, and divinity. I had prayed for her every day there. But since Sarah's birth, I hadn't been back.

Two weeks later, while the boys were in school, I grabbed a book I had just been given, *I Am Your Jesus of Mercy*, which contained messages Mary was reported to have given, placed Sarah in her car seat, and drove to our church. There in the adoration prayer chapel I found myself alone with my baby. My heart was in anguish and I cried out to Jesus, "Please, I need to know that this is your will. I need to know that there is some reason for all of this. I can't imagine why I would be asked to have another child with the same diagnosis. If there is something in this book that will let me know this is what you truly desire, that this *is* your will, let me open to it now." I didn't normally trust those kind of random choices, but I felt desperate for direction and a word from God about this whole messed-up ordeal.

I randomly opened the book and read:

My dear little children, praise be Jesus!
My little ones, please do not be afraid or confused.

My plan for you is great.
It is one of joy and freedom.
Unite in me in prayer for my plan....
Only God visualizes the plan in its entirety, and you, little
    children, must remain dependent on Him, trusting in His
    divine will.
As God's will unfolds daily, please do not be sad or confused
    when you realize His will may not be what you have
    planned.
Remain open and accept His plan for you with unconditional
    love.
God's works are wondrous.
He confuses the proud and exalts the humble.
Surrender to His will in peace.
It will result in eternal happiness, for God will remain faithful
    to His promise.
Bless you, little children.
I take your petitions to the Sacred Heart of Jesus.
Bless you!
Thank you for responding to my call,
Ad Deum

A quiet calm came over me. I took a deep breath as peace began to flow through me. The sorrow was still there, but to know this was God's will was everything. He desired that Sarah be born with SMA, and that her life be short. I thanked Jesus for answering me, and I prayed for the strength and grace I needed to get through this next journey.

Sarah, despite her diagnosis, was the joy of our lives. The boys loved to play with her and make her laugh, which didn't take much; she was always happy. As usual, Drew treated her like a princess.

But it didn't take long for us to see the signs of SMA developing. Her legs that were once so strong began to languish. Her arms grew weak as well, and she never held her head up. She, as her sister Kelly, loved to lie flat on the table. She was still able to roll her head from side to side, and she absolutely loved watching her brothers run around the house and play. They in turn loved playing with her and making her laugh. Her smile would light up the room, and her eyes were gentle and full of love, with that same ability to look deep past you and into your soul as Kelly's had.

I returned to my daily visits to the chapel, always taking Sarah with me. It was in that place that I gained greater peace and strength. One morning, when Sarah was about three months, while we were in front of the tabernacle, I heard Jesus ask me to return to Medjugorje. Even more, I felt he wanted me first to go on a retreat with Father Sudac, the Croatian priest with the stigmata, or crucifixion wounds of Christ, and then on to Medjugorje.

A tremendous burden came over me as I heard this request. Not again. This was too much! I did not want to go. And I was so, so tired.

"I don't want to go, Jesus. I've given birth to two children thirteen months apart. I have buried one and I am going to soon have to bury another. I am so weary. Please don't ask me to go."

You aren't going to deny me, are you? he replied simply.

His words cut me deeply. I tried so hard not to disobey Christ. I'd failed so many times, but I never willingly wanted to deny him anything. With a heavy heart, I answered back. "No, I will not deny you. If this is what you want, I'll go."

I couldn't understand why God wanted me to make another trip to Medjugorje. I didn't need it for my faith, as I had on my previous trips. I didn't doubt God or his will. I simply could not see the reason to go.

Drew was surprised when I told him what I had heard in prayer, and he wanted to know if I would be taking Sarah. It had crossed my mind briefly, but I told him, no, Sarah would stay home. I would not seek Sarah's healing.

CHAPTER 25

Return to Medjugorje

Five months later, my friend Martha and I joined up with Mike and Sandy Tobin's group, whom I'd traveled with on my first venture. Our group of thirty Americans teamed up with thirty Croatians for Father Zlatko Sudac's retreat at Mali Lošinj, on one of the many islands in the Adriatic Sea off the west coast of Croatia. In the past, Father Sudac had traveled abroad to speak at various conferences, but recently he'd been restricted by his bishop only to minister from this retreat house. He had also been asked to keep the cross-shaped wound he had mystically received on his forehead covered with bandages.

Father Sudac greeted us all for the first time, a young man with shoulder-length dark hair and a short, well-kept mustache and beard. The flesh-colored bandages over the center of his forehead were barely noticeable. Around his wrists were wrapped white bands of fabric that he had artistically embellished, covering the wounds there. All of this was in obedience to his bishop's orders.

We learned later that Father Sudac was a prolific and talented artist in many mediums. The Bethany Retreat House, where he lived, was filled with his paintings, mosaics, and stained glass work. He humbly greeted us and welcomed us to the house. Our stay would be for seven days, during which he would lead us in several meditation sessions per day. Daily mass was provided, along with time for confession. Though no one was scheduled to meet with Father Sudac privately, he would pray individually over each of us.

To be in the presence of such a holy man was inspiring. At our first mass with him, I sat in the front, interested to hear his message. When he got up to speak, he looked at me for a moment and then said, as though he were speaking only to me, "All suffering has meaning. Especially the suffering of little children, the holy innocents." Then he started his homily. I didn't follow the rest of what he said, because I was lost in thought. Suffering had meaning. My girls' lives had meaning. I really needed to hear that. Even though we know these things, as humans we so often need to be reminded and reassured. I was in that place that day. I needed the reassurance that only God knew the end result of my daughters' suffering, and that they were playing a part in his overall plan. That was the only question I'd brought with me for Father Sudac, and it was answered the first day.

Throughout the retreat, as people learned of my story, they all responded with the same remark: "You need to ask for her healing."

But I was at a different place in my life now. After walking with Kelly through her brief life and now expecting the same with

Sarah, I had come to look differently at death. I had come to see it as a gift. Death is probably the greatest gift God can give us, because unless we die, we cannot be with him in heaven, and that is where all of us were meant to be. While it was sure to bring me great pain, I was okay with Sarah dying because I knew she would ultimately be with God in heaven. She would experience what she was truly created for.

Despite this, it seemed as though most everything I heard on the retreat had to do with healing. Every talk, every homily, and now different people telling me to pray for Sarah's healing. I never felt that Sarah was to be healed and I had never once asked for Sarah's healing. Yet here I was, hearing so much about healing. I began to think that perhaps the reason I had been asked to go on the retreat was in fact to ask for this miracle. Perhaps she was supposed to be an image of God's mercy to the world.

In one homily Father Sudac explained why we don't see the healings and miracles today that the early church experienced during the time of the apostles: because there isn't enough faith.

"If you want a miracle," he said, "you should pray, fast, prepare, and then ask. Ask without leaving any room for doubt, and then, immediately begin giving thanks, acting in your heart as if the miracle has already occurred. Thank the Lord every day for your miracle, whether it takes two weeks or fifteen years." He went on to tell us of a miracle that had occurred in which a woman in a wheelchair thanked God for her healing every day for fifteen years—a healing that didn't seem to be happening—until one day she stood up out of the wheelchair and walked.

I believed God could heal Sarah; I just didn't know if it was his will. But maybe I was supposed to ask for it—especially because Sarah had already almost outlived her life expectancy. She was supposed to live only nine months, as Kelly had. But when I left for the retreat, Sarah was already eight months old and showed no evidence of significant problems aside from the fact she was weak. Maybe that was why I was on this retreat. I didn't ever want to look back and think I had missed an opportunity to save my daughter. I couldn't live with that. So I thought of what Father Sudac had said. Pray, fast, prepare, and then ask without doubt. I was already on retreat, praying intensely. I couldn't pray any harder. I always prayed that God's will be done in Sarah's life. I had fasted while seeking God's will in Sarah's life. My next step was to prepare. The following day in the adoration chapel, I asked for Sarah's healing. I asked with all my heart, left no room for doubt, and from that moment on I began to thank God for my miracle. Every day I thanked God for healing Sarah.

At the conclusion of our retreat, we traveled to Medjugorje. Saying goodbye to our new Croatian friends, we boarded a ferry and traveled overnight to Split, Croatia, where we climbed on our bus for the three-hour ride into the village.

It was my third trip there. I could never have imagined I would return after my first trip, but here I was, showing everyone around Medjugorje. It was a wonderful and relaxing time. Again, I felt as if I had found a little piece of heaven. While many in our group saw the miracle of the sun, I was content simply to enjoy the peace and joy that pervaded the village. All the while, I continued to thank Jesus for Sarah's healing, sure now that it would come. Just not sure what it would look like.

CHAPTER 26

Enjoying Sarah

I returned home after two weeks of being away. It felt good to have my family throw their arms around me and make me promise never to go away again for so long, and I happily agreed.

I had continued to thank our Lord for Sarah's healing, and as I journeyed home, I became eager to see her again. When I took Sarah in my arms for the first time after being back, I suddenly felt a gentle push from one of her legs. She had not moved her legs in months!

Day by day, we continued to notice that her muscles were strengthening slightly. She began to move her arms, her legs, and even tried to hold her head up. Little by little she was growing stronger. She began to eat solid food, something her sister, Kelly, had never been able to do.

For several months, we continued to enjoy Sarah's strengthening. Her healing and the joy she brought into our lives was incredible. Laughter filled the house and we took Sarah with us on all our outings to the boys' sporting events, as well as walks along the beach. Her doctors were amazed. They never expected her to live so long, much less have this gentle, growing strength.

We began to make plans again. For the first time in years, we were not worried. The stress was gone and our future looked bright.

Then one day about six months later, we noticed Sarah stopped moving her legs. Slowly, all other strength left her, until her hands were all she could move. She had trouble eating and soon went back on formula feedings. After seeing Kelly go through her demise, we watched in anguish as Sarah continued to weaken. While she had been laughing only weeks earlier, now she could barely smile. She could now communicate only through her eyes.

Sarah, like Kelly, developed a cold and required hospitalization for the pneumonia she developed in her lungs. There she was given IV antibiotics, oxygen, and aggressive breathing and suctioning treatments. Air was forced into her lungs to expand them for her, because she was too feeble to take the deep breaths necessary to keep them fully open. A tube was placed through her nose and into her stomach, so she could receive the nutrition she couldn't swallow.

Eventually, Sarah needed to be placed on a ventilator, a machine that would breathe for her. While it had never been a true option for Kelly, the doctors felt Sarah would benefit from the short period of rest she would be allowed by not having to struggle to breathe and perhaps allow her to fight off her lung infection. For several days we never knew if Sarah would survive, much less be strong enough ever again to breathe on her own.

We continued to pray. One early morning Drew went for a run on the beach. When he returned, his hands were filled with six perfect sand dollars. He seemed happy.

"Wow!" I was impressed that he'd found so many. As a family we loved to look for sand dollars on the beach but could never find a perfect one. And here he came with six!

"Guess what, Cyndi?" he told me excitedly. "While I ran, I prayed about Sarah and her future. I told God that ever since you returned from Medjugorje and began to claim Sarah's healing, I have embraced that and am grateful for how the Holy Spirit has been growing my faith and leading us as a family. But I've never asked for a sign, as you have. While I was running, I came across a broken sand dollar." He smiled. "I figured I'd ask for a sign, so I asked him to give me three perfect sand dollars to show me that he is there and he is listening. I took about ten more steps, and I ran into one, then two, then *three*, then *four*, then *five*, and then *six*." He exhaled in delight. "I knew then that God was truly wrapping us in his arms. And while I was picking them up, I had this incredible calm come over me."

I joined his delight. I was amazed and in awe that God was moving so clearly in Drew's life too.

Finally within a few days Sarah gained her strength, now that she no longer struggled to breathe, and she began to fight the pneumonia that had settled into her lungs. She did make it back off the ventilator and after struggling in the hospital for a few weeks, she grew strong enough to fight off the infection and recover. She was allowed to go home, but only on hospice care.

Sarah continued her feeding through the tube that ran into her stomach, and we continued the breathing treatments. She did well considering her condition. And she loved being back in her home with the brothers she adored. While she could no longer laugh at them, her faint smile and bright eyes told us of her joy.

Her life and ours became one of nonstop care. Again, like Kelly, she required another hospitalization, where she only partially improved. With nothing left for the hospital to offer us, we took her home. She continued on, under our aggressive monitoring and treatment. Sarah had also been given the same type of oxygen saturation monitor that Kelly had, which measured the amount of oxygen in her blood. Whenever it dropped too low, the alarm would sound and we would run into her room to start another breathing treatment. It was something we had grown used to. Every two to three hours, day and night around the clock, we would have to treat her again. After several months of this, we were sleep deprived and worn, but happy and grateful she was alive. Sarah was twenty-one months old. She had already lived well past what the medical community believed was possible.

Late one night in December 2004, her dad snuck into her room and played with her for almost an hour, watching her wave her lightest toy and barely smile, as he played peek-a-boo. Kissing Sarah goodnight and then making sure her monitor was in place, he left.

The next morning, I was startled to discover I awoke on my own. It was strange that the alarm had not gone off as we had expected. But it had felt good to get a full night's sleep. I couldn't even remember the last time I had slept all the way to the morning. Drew awoke too and began to tell me how happy Sarah had been last night with him. We got up and walked together to her room to check on her.

We found her blue and barely breathing... with her monitor in place. It had not sounded, even though it was registering an oxygen level significantly below normal. We tried to revive her, but quickly knew it was hopeless. Not wanting to cause her any more pain, I picked her up and gently cradled her in my arms, while Drew called for her brothers to come.

And once again, I helplessly held another child as she passed away.

As I clutched the body of my daughter, I couldn't help but ask the same question that had plagued me over and over. *Why?*

I didn't understand. I knew we had been asked to have this baby and truly I was glad we did. I loved Sarah and couldn't imagine life without her ever having been in it. She put so much love in our home, in all of our lives. She grounded our growing faith. And now she too was gone. She had joined her sister.

I gently bathed her, outfitted her in a soft pink dress, wrapped her body in a blanket, and then while Socorro kept the boys, Drew and I took Sarah's small body to the adoration chapel in our church. There we laid her at the feet of Jesus. She was his now. She had always been his, but now she was in his eternal presence. Our pastor found us and tried to comfort us. He prayed over Sarah's body and blessed her. Finally, after thirty minutes, Drew gently picked her up and we returned home.

With this child, I took my time in saying goodbye, calling the funeral home only when all of us were as ready as we were ever going to be to let her go. They wrapped her gently in her blanket and carried her to the waiting car. As I watched them take her away, I felt confused. Sarah had gotten stronger, but ultimately, it was God's will that she leave us.

Why, God? I asked. *Why give me hope only to take it away?*

CHAPTER 27

Questions for God

Two days later, I nursed my grief and anger. And was I ever angry. I relished in it. I felt I'd earned the right to be upset.

What was the whole point? Why did God seem like a cruel trickster? I pray for healing and he gives Sarah strength, but then takes it away. Why give me the hope when she was still going to die?

Is God really all-powerful? I wondered. I couldn't rely on medicine. And now it appeared that I couldn't rely on God either. All that was left was a sense of feeling lost. So I would do what I'd always done in the past—rely on myself. I may not be all-powerful but at least I could trust myself.

I didn't understand God's role in my life any more. And I was tired of asking for clarity. So this was it. I was done. No more praying. Obviously, it hadn't worked before—at least not the way I felt it should have—so it was time for me to quit.

The funeral was approaching. We'd set a time for it a week later so that extended family could make arrangements to attend. The closer it got, the more confused and frustrated I felt. I knew people would expect me to say something at the funeral, just as I had at Kelly's. But I had nothing to say. What *could* I say when I didn't understand anything?

Finally after a few more days, I was at the end of myself. Harboring resentment didn't bring back my daughter. It didn't make me a more fulfilled and joyful person. It certainly didn't help me grieve. It only brought more pain.

Cyndi, you're too smart to let this go too long, I told myself. *If you let it go too long, your anger will eat you up and it will destroy you, and you don't want that. So stop what you're doing. Just stop. Grow up. Quit being a child and grow up.*

I knew the cure, as much as I wanted to refuse it. I needed to go to the adoration chapel. I needed to go to Jesus. Even in all my anger, he was the only place I could go for help.

When I arrived at our parish, I saw my pastor. He approached me with words of comfort and then began to discuss the upcoming funeral.

"I know I have to say something," I told him. "But I don't have anything to say. I'm at a loss."

"Why would you think that people are expecting something from you?"

"I just know they are. And I know that God wants me to say something, but I have nothing to say. And I'm angry."

He nodded his understanding. "You know, Cyndi, it's okay to be angry with God. He can handle it. Give him everything you've got. He's much bigger than your anger. And he gave you the emotion of anger for a reason. He's not afraid of it."

His words gave me the strength to walk into that chapel.

Slowly I entered the chapel and knelt. In my mind there was nothing God could tell me to help me understand. He had taken my hope, and my daughter, away from me. I was broken. Pierced through. Again.

I looked at the gold box, or what we call the tabernacle, that housed the consecrated hosts—the bread for communion. I knew it represented the same tabernacle in the Holy of holies that housed the manna that God gave to the Israelites as they wandered through the desert for forty years. Because the gold box held the consecrated hosts, I knew it was truly Jesus, the true bread that came down from heaven. It was Jesus whom I needed right then.

"You have... *failed* me." My words came out quietly but with so much emotion. You asked me to have this child and I did. I went on the retreat. I prayed for healing. Thank you for the months of joy with Sarah—they were great. But why strengthen her like that, if you were just going to take her in the end? I was okay with her dying, but you gave me hope she would live. You gave me that hope. Why? You *failed* me."

Then I heard a quiet voice inside of me say, *Have I failed you? How have I failed you? I have answered every true prayer of your heart.*

I sat stunned. That was the last thing I thought I would hear.

What were the true prayers of my heart? I wondered. They came to me almost instantly, and I don't think they are any different from those of most mothers. I wanted my husband and my children to have a living, breathing faith. The truest prayers of my heart were that my family deeply believe in God so that we would all go to heaven.

I thought of my girls. They were in heaven. I really didn't have anything to do with that but I did have three boys for whom I was accountable. I had the responsibility to grow and shape them with the mind and heart of Jesus Christ. I had the responsibility for my husband's soul as well.

I was drawn back to my retreat with Father Sudac. It was only then that I remembered what he had said about miracles: "If you do not get your miracle, you need to pray. Pray to understand why that cross has been placed in your life, and left in your life. What are the graces you needed, which only that cross could bring to you?"

What were the graces we needed from the short lives of Kelly and Sarah? Immediately, the answers flooded my mind.

First, I needed grace to cover my pride. I'd always felt that I could handle anything that anybody threw at me. Nothing was going to get me down. I could beat it. And I could—except for the death of my children. There was nothing I could do. My daughters' afflictions had stopped me in my tracks and made me face the questions head on: Is Jesus real? And if he is, then what am I doing about it? What am I doing to make him the center of my life?

I looked at the way I'd lived before those girls and I hadn't done a thing to make Jesus the center of my life. I was striving to be a prominent dermatologic surgeon. And what was I doing to lead my children to Christ? Absolutely nothing. I was leading them to live a life in which the important things were really money, status, and career. But only through the death of these two children, by stopping me cold and facing the questions head on, did I realize what the most important thing is in life: having a relationship with Christ. Money, career, status—all those things are fleeting and fickle. It's the eternal that never changes, that impacts us and strengthens families and allows love to thrive. Because of my daughters I needed all that time with them to learn how to pray, to get close to Christ, to bring my husband closer to Christ, to bring my children to Jesus, to change the way I lived. None of that would have happened—I'm sorry to say, since I'm pretty thick—without the death of a child.

Kelly had given me the courage to talk to my husband about my faith, and because of that we were then able to live our faith in our family. We prayed together every night as a family. We attended weekly mass as a family. My boys had become altar servers. I was taking my children to confession and adoration. We reviewed Scripture together every week. All of that was because of the lives of my daughters. They gave us the strength and the courage and the energy to pursue God.

I looked at myself and realized I had become that mom I wanted to be. I did bless my children with holy water. I had crucifixes in all of their bedrooms. Our house was blessed. I let them find me praying my rosary. We lit blessed candles together and we spoke of God every day. I had become the mother I truly wanted to be on my first trip to Medjugorje.

And I began speaking to others. I spoke at parishes, prayer groups, and conferences about my life with my daughters and the changes they had brought to my family and so many others. At first I was terrified, and it is always painful to relive the memories, but I realize there are graces that come to others in hearing about Kelly and Sarah. Many people are touched and write me letters saying how their faith has been so affected and deepened by what they have heard. One woman even wrote to tell me she named her newborn daughter Sarah Kelly in remembrance of my daughters.

Every prayer I had prayed on Apparition Hill my first morning in Medjugorje had been answered. My husband and children were living lives that honored God, and other souls were being brought to Jesus through the lives of Kelly and Sarah, because I was speaking out about my faith.

Those two little girls did that. They brought our lives from ones centered on the world and all it had to offer, to ones centered on Christ. I don't think anything but their lives could have done that.

"But why did they have to die?" I whispered to him. "A miracle would have caused so many people to believe in you."

He answered gently. *Your faith in me, despite the loss of two of your daughters, speaks louder than any miracle ever could.*

CHAPTER 28

Another Funeral

E ven with God's guidance, my heart ached. I understood it was his will, but it did not lessen the pain and the void I felt inside. While we never fully understand the will of God, we are asked to trust. I trust that God needed my daughters to live the lives they did and to join him in heaven when they did. While on this side of eternity I will never completely understand why, I do trust.

I knew God wanted me to speak at Sarah's funeral, but I couldn't. For three days I tried to think of something, anything, to say, but my mind and my heart were empty.

By the eve of the funeral, I still feared that I would step onto the platform and stare out at the group with nothing to say. My family and I attended the visitation at the church. Sarah had an open casket and just as Kelly had, she wore a little wreath of roses on her head. I was amazed by how many people showed up. Kids from Drew and John's school came and dropped little toys into the casket. And we had placed construction paper in the back of the church so that the kids could make little cards and color and draw pictures for Sarah.

A woman from our parish led everyone in the rosary. It was touching. As I lingered through the visitation and heard person after person offer their love and condolences, a heavy burden continued to sit squarely on my shoulders: I still wasn't sure what I would speak on the next day at the funeral.

A few hours before I was about to retire for the night, God's spirit moved over me with words. I jumped up and ran to find paper and jotted everything down. The words flowed quickly. They were everything I'd wanted to say but didn't know how. God had provided strength again.

The next day, I once again watched my husband and several pallbearers carry the child-sized coffin down the center aisle of our church. Our oldest son, Drew Jr., read again for this funeral—this time he gave the first reading from the book of Habakkuk, chapter 2, about a man who complains to God and desires an answer. God responds to him by saying he is to wait for his answer, that it will come, and it will not be late.

After Drew finished, our second son, John, got up to read. He was now old enough and had begged to give the second reading. He read from St. Paul's letter to the Romans, chapter 8, about how our sufferings in this time are nothing compared to the glory that awaits us and that God uses everything for the good and for his glory. And Jack, now six years old, was able to join as well, and he helped to carry down the gifts of bread and wine to our pastor.

John's third-grade class from school sang. They all had known Sarah well and had volunteered to sing in the choir. They wanted to honor her life in some way. Their young voices blending together in praise to God was beautiful and moving.

Drew then approached the lectern and spoke in-depth about the importance of family prayer, citing a statistic the international author and speaker Matthew Kelly had used, that one of every two marriages will end in divorce, but of the families that pray together, only one in two thousand end in divorce. Drew spoke lovingly of Sarah and how much she would be missed in our lives.

I listened in awe. God truly had worked a miracle: my husband had a strong faith.

My turn came and, once again, I took the podium. I knew exactly what I wanted to say. I pulled out my notes and laid them across the podium.

"Look around you," I said, not feeling nervous, as I had when I'd begun at Kelly's funeral. This time my voice felt sure and strong. "Look at how many people are here. This little girl has touched all of your lives. Not even two years old, not strong enough to sit up on her own. What is it that touched you?

"Sarah was such a little light. She loved to smile, and she loved to laugh, and she loved to play peek-a-boo. Her favorite toy was a balloon. Her brothers, Drew, John, and Jack, all loved to make her laugh. She would brighten up whenever they came into the room, and she always watched them."

I glanced down at Drew and continued. "Her dad was the joy of her life." As I said the words, a tight smile crossed his face and he nodded slightly. "Every day, he would rush in the house, scoop her up, and they would be off for a visit to someone, a walk, or a swim in the pool. She never left his side.

"We all wanted Sarah to live. Many of you know I believed she would be healed. It didn't happen. This is God's will. I accept it. And I pray that God's will is always done in my life, because I know it is best, and I trust him. But I look around here and I wonder, what is the greater miracle? The healing of a little girl, or the effect she had on your faith? If just one person was brought closer to Christ through our belief that Sarah could be healed, or anything that we said along the way, then I would go through it all again and not change one single thing, not even the outcome. A life with Christ at the center is the most important thing we can strive for. If Sarah has brought you closer on that path, her life had tremendous value.

"God only wants one thing from us: to grow in his love. The purpose of our life on earth is to become the best version of ourselves. To become what he envisioned when he created us. He will send us gifts to help us along. I see Sarah as such a gift. She is God's little way of getting us or keeping us on the path to him, to choose to grow in love to him.

"Sarah made us look at our lives—individually and as a family—and ask: What is it that we truly want out of life? That's the bottom line. When it is all said and done, what is it? And then we must ask: How do we make that happen?

"Matthew Kelly has said: 'Tell me your habits, and I'll tell you your life. Tell me your habits, and I'll tell you where your life is going. Tell me your habits, and I'll tell you what you truly value.'

"The death of my first daughter, Kelly, made me look at my life. My heart's desire was to be as close to Jesus as I possibly could, and yet I wasn't doing a thing to make that happen. I needed to change my habits.

"Through Sarah, we looked at the habits of our family and realized we needed to cultivate habits that would make Jesus the center of our lives. So we began family habits, to help us grow in love to Christ.

"Many of you know Mary is special to me. She is the Mother of God. I listened to her and I realized that she truly is my mother. And like any good mother, she will always point us in the direction our lives should go. Mary always points us to her Son. And like a good mother, she shows us how.

"I first began to live her messages that she'd given at Medjugorje, through the short life of Kelly. And my family has begun to live the messages throughout my daughter Sarah's life. Both of them have brought Christ into our lives. If any of you see our family and recognize there is something that you want, it is simply the presence and grace of God.

"Mary's messages are simple: to change your habits. She gives us five ways to do so.

"The first is through conversion, to choose Christ and to mean it.

"The second is to pray. Mary asks us to pray the rosary every day. I don't know why she has chosen the rosary. All I know is that she is the Mother of God and she has asked this. I trust her. I have prayed the rosary every day for four years now. It is my habit.

"We pray every night together as a family. We don't let it slip. If someone is sleeping, we pray around them and for them. Usually one decade of the rosary. It is our habit, and this is the most important habit. If you commit to prayer, God will show you where to turn next.

"The third is reconciliation. Mary asks us to go to confession once a month. Drew and I have made this our habit. We need to make it our family habit.

"The fourth is to receive Christ as often as possible. At first, I started to go to mass just one more day per week outside of Sunday. Now I go every day, and Drew tries to do the same. If we can't make it, we visit the adoration chapel, where Christ is always present. It is our habit.

"The fifth is fasting. Mary asks us to give up something on Wednesdays and Fridays. I started by turning off my radio, then the television. If you don't take the noise out of your life, you will never hear God. I slowly gave up more and more on these two days every week. Give up something. It keeps your mind on Christ and opens your heart to him.

"Your children can fast too. All of my kids have fasted for Sarah. Jack has given up his popsicles; Drew, watching sports; and John, his television time. When you give of yourself, you grow in love. You allow God to enter into you.

"The final message is to choose peace. Peace in everything—peace in your own heart, your family, and in those who surround you. As Saint Pio has said: 'Peace, peace, and only peace.'

"These are Mary's messages. Her guidance. We have made them our habits. They have brought us a deep peace and comfort. They have brought Jesus into our lives. And like the man who builds his house on a foundation of rock, when the challenges come, although they bring us pain, they never bring us despair. We have that peace.

"That was the gift of Sarah and Kelly. They made us stop our lives and truly confront the issues straight on. Is Christ real? And if so, what are we doing to bring ourselves and those we love closer to him?

"Sarah challenges us to look at our lives. Where are we going? What are our habits? Are they leading us to Christ? If so, what are they? And if not, why not?

"God wants you to become the best version of yourself. He will send you gifts to keep you on that path. Sarah is such a gift. Thank you, Sarah."

I concluded and looked out to the crowd of silent onlookers. Everyone was staring at me and the room felt dead quiet. My heart sank. Had I made any sense at all?

I sat next to Drew and waited for the choir to sing again, but the choir director simply sat at the piano with her fingers sitting still on the keys. Finally, I saw her move to sit a little straighter and then she began to play. The choir sang a special version of "Ave Maria" that is popular in Medjugorje. She knew the version was meaningful to me because of where it had originated. And then each of them presented me with a rose.

At the end of the funeral Drew stood and with the other pallbearers, mostly our brothers, he led them with the coffin back up the center aisle and into the hearse that waited.

And for a second time, it was over.

CHAPTER 29

A Mother's Vision

One year after Sarah's death, I felt called to return to Medjugorje. I'd had a difficult year. The pain of my wounds still lingered, and although God had been a faithful, comforting companion—and I now had my depression in check, and life was moving on—my arms still ached to hold the children I'd been forced to hand over to death. But the tug to return to the mystical place I'd visited for the first time five years before became more pronounced. I kept getting a vision of a healing balm being rubbed over my heart. It was almost as if God were calling me to that place in order to heal me. While the tug was gentle, I felt no insistent pressure as I had in my previous visits. It was there for my decision. If I chose to go, I knew that I would find peace, but if I chose not to visit, I would be okay as well. So my expectations for anything spectacular or miraculous were fairly low. I assumed God was offering me the opportunity to have some down time.

This time I went with a new group and stayed with the visionary Mirjana. I wanted to be with a group who didn't know my story, who wouldn't offer me pity or try to comfort me. I simply wanted to be alone. Going back to all of the familiar sites brought joy and comfort to my heart. And although I didn't participate in many of the group activities, since I'd done everything before, I welcomed the solitude and spent most of my time there in prayer. Every morning I rose and headed up Apparition Hill, where I prayed and meditated. Then I attended mass with the group and went to confession.

One day, about halfway through the trip, I was walking along the red dusty path that wound back into town to meet up with three fun women from my group. At one point I casually glanced up to the top of Apparition Hill and instantly felt pulled to climb the hill. Only, I didn't want to. I'd already climbed it that morning, plus the afternoon sun made the day very hot. If I climbed now, I would get all sweaty, and I had just showered. Besides, I was supposed to meet the women I was traveling with.

I continued toward town, but again the call came to climb. I stopped and began to talk myself out of it, when a third time the thought came: *Climb Apparition Hill.* Suddenly I realized I was being an idiot. I had traveled halfway around the world because I was asked to go on this trip. If my heart told me to climb the hill, I should climb the hill!

I headed toward the hill and began the ascent. The path was dusty and crowded with people, making me even hotter and sweatier. Groups were dotted along the hillside, praying their rosaries, all in different languages, led by their tour guides on loudspeakers. I skirted around these groups and around a few older women and men slowly making the climb with walking sticks.

Finally I made it about halfway to the top, near the statue of Our Lady of Medjugorje. I diverged from the mass of people surrounding her, and found a quiet spot with a large, flat rock to sit on. As I settled down, I noticed my shoe was untied and my mind traveled back to that day in the gym when I had given my heart to Christ.

That's funny, because this thing kind of all started with my shoe being untied and me being asked to say I love you to Jesus.

Then it hit me. Through all the time with Kelly and Sarah I had never truly consecrated my family to Jesus and Mary. I closed my eyes, went deep inside my heart, and prayed for Jesus and Mary always to watch over my family as I gave them, one by one, fully over to them.

When I finished, I opened my eyes. As I glanced toward the top of the hill, I saw Mary. She was clothed in a gray dress with her mantle over her head. In her arms were my daughters, one on each side. Mary's glance locked with mine. In an instant, my daughters were gone and now Mary held the dead body of her Son, Jesus, draped over her arms.

The pain of loss clutched my stomach at the sight. All my questioning and accusations that Jesus had failed me now faced me in this image.

As she looked at me, I heard her words, spoken softly and gently: *Why did your daughters have to die? Why did my Son have to die? It was a sacrifice only you and I could offer.*

And then they were gone.

CHAPTER 30

Discovering the Miracles

If I wondered how my daughters' lives could ever have meaning and make a difference in the world, I didn't have long to find out. For months afterward, I discovered that my children and my words at the final funeral service had caused dozens of people to turn to their faith, to pray more intentionally, and to grow closer to their families, realizing no one really knows how much time they have with their children.

I received countless cards and letters from people who were either at the funeral or had heard about our story. Messages such as this one gave me strength and reminded me that God never wastes our pain:

> It's easy to get angry and resentful, and that's how I felt when I walked into St. James on Saturday. But your resolution in your faith in God helped even me get past my anger—it gave

me strength in my faith. I took what you said to heart; so now instead of rushing through our bedtime prayers, we stop and reflect on what we are asking for and what we are thankful for. And as my faith in God deepens, and my children's faith grows, I must thank you for your strength and your two beautiful angels.

I saw my husband's faith continue to grow. Throughout the entire experience, Drew wrote letters to his daughters. With each letter, his faith and trust in God became more evident. In fact, after the funeral, a woman approached me and asked, "Was it hard for your husband to choose between married life and becoming a priest?" My first thought was, *What? My husband? The one who never wanted to go to church and wanted to stay home and make breakfast?* But then I realized how many steps forward he'd taken in his faith. God had answered my prayers for a strong husband. A miracle.

I also saw that initial vision of my speaking come true. I'd fought it so hard and so long, and after my daughters died, I realized speaking in front of people about my faith was no longer the scary proposition I'd first considered it to be. I'd complained that I didn't have a story to tell. Well, I definitely had a story now! One of faithfulness and trust. And one of miracles that are all around us. We just need to look for them with different eyes and perspectives.

As speaking engagements came, I found myself excitedly clinging to any moment when I could share what God had done in our lives. My girls had empowered *me* to be able to speak in front of people about spiritual things—that which I had feared most of all. Groups were now asking me to address them and testify to how someone could ever go on after losing a child and do so with such grace and faith, while strengthening their marriage and family. Marriages were supposed to fall apart after losing a child, not grow deeper. Those were all miracles.

And finally the day came that I'd specifically seen in my vision: me standing behind a microphone on a stage in front of five thousand people. When I stepped onto the stage to take my spot, I looked out and realized, *This is it. It's happened, and I'm not afraid. I'm thrilled to be here.* God knew what he was doing all along. I think he knew I would end up speaking not because I had to, but because I wanted to, because I wanted to devote myself to him and to bring other people to him. So that day on Apparition Hill in Medjugorje when I'd asked God to remove this terrible vision from me, he'd agreed. And I believe it really was okay if I didn't speak, but he knew that I *would want* to, that everything within me wanted to share God with anyone who would listen. Another miracle.

Our grief continued, but God offered comfort throughout the days and months that passed. When Kelly died, we grieved, but we were able to pour our energies and hopes and love into our new child, Sarah. With Sarah's death, we had no more new children, and had to rely completely and utterly on God. It wasn't that I wasn't grateful for my other children—I was! And I poured myself into being the best mother I could. And again God proved a faithful companion and friend. Especially when I learned that I could have no more children, since I went through premature menopause during Sarah's brief time with us.

I could have wallowed in self-pity. And to be honest, that's how my life and faith used to be—totally self-centered. I used to pray constantly for and about myself. When I first started this

journey, it was all about me and me, me, me. *Make me stronger.*
Make me have more faith. But now I find my prayers are for others.
I see a world in desperate need of Jesus and that consumes most
of my prayer focus.

"Why?" had been my biggest question throughout the entire
experience.

There's a story about St. Augustine, in which he was going to
figure out God and the Holy Trinity. He spent years formulating
theories and explanations for the mystery of the Trinity. One day
while walking along the beach, he came upon a boy who had dug a
small hole in the sand. The boy kept running back to the sea with
a seashell, filling it with water and then returning to the beach to
dump the water into the hole.

Augustine watched the boy's comings and goings for some
time and then approached him about it.

"What are you doing?" he asked.

"I'm fitting the entire sea in this hole."

"Young boy, you will never fit the entire sea in that hole. It's an
impossible task."

To which the boy replied, "And so is trying to figure out God."

Augustine was so taken with the boy's response that he looked
away to ponder it. When he looked back toward the boy, he was
gone.

I have that same feeling about this entire experience. I can
spend my whole life wondering, *Why? Why? Why?* And I will
never figure out why, other than that it was meant to be. And
that is enough for me. So I'm content. The truth is that while I
will always want the answer, I don't need to have it. I just need to
live the life God has called me to—with its joys and its sorrows—
knowing that he wastes neither in his work to make us more

like Christ. And someday when I join my daughters in heaven, I will know. Everything will be answered and I will see the bigger picture—and I will rejoice in the suffering that we experienced here on earth.

I have been blessed. I have a family who loves God and pursues him. I speak and write about my story—God's story. And I've even begun leading groups to Medjugorje and have now been there more than a dozen times. I find great satisfaction in watching others discover the God who is for us and never against us. And I love hearing their stories once they return home, of their changed lives and families. My life is fuller and more complete than it ever has been. I have joy—the kind that doesn't fade and that is content with knowing God is in control. None of this would have happened had it not been for the suffering. And that is yet another miracle.

I spent so much time waiting for a miracle—a miracle of my own determination. Ultimately, though, the miracle of healing I sought became a miracle in dozens of other ways, for which I am grateful. Through the suffering, I discovered the satisfaction and completeness I had always longed for. And I was finally able to rest in the knowledge that nothing happens outside of his control and he allows all things—even the most difficult—for our ultimate good. Because of my experiences I have changed for the better. I am now at peace and no longer struggle with the empty longing I used to feel. I've discovered that God is good. All the time. And even when we believe he has failed us, what we do not see is that he is vigilantly working behind the scenes on our behalf. Always.

I have definitely been blessed by special graces from God, but I am no more loved or holy than anyone else. And Christ prepared me for a difficult time in my life and for a mission. And that mission is to be a witness to the fact that God is very real, and that a personal relationship with him is possible for everyone. All we need to do is accept Jesus as our savior and acknowledge that we need his saving grace and work in our lives, and then we begin to live out of obedience and love for him. When we place Christ at the center of our lives and at the center of our very souls, then we will know he is there. Not by visions or messages, but by the peace that enters our lives.

While early in my faith journey, I needed pronounced miracles, such as the rosary beads turning gold and viewing the miracle of the sun, as a constant reassurance that God is real, I no longer need them. I realize that my experience with miracles may never be the same as what others experience; God may not need to go to such lengths to get others' attention as he needed to with me. But when we look for God's hand at work in our lives, we *can* see his miraculous fingerprints everywhere. Reminding us that he is faithful, that suffering is never wasted when we trust him, and that joy really does come through the journey. And that is a miracle I'm more than willing and ready to wait for.

APPENDIX A

Reflections on Waiting for a Miracle

Although this book tells my story, I don't want it to stop there. This book is really a place for you to consider your own journey and God's purpose for your life. In this appendix, you'll find reflection questions based on the themes and challenges that I faced as a point of reference in the hope that as you answer the questions, you will enter your own discovery process about faith, struggles, obedience, grief, redemption, meaning, and joy.

Feel free to use this guide in your individual study or with a book club or small faith group to help spark discussion.

Chapter 1: Pleading for a Miracle

❖ Are there areas in your life where you need a miracle? What are they? If you could pick the miracle and how it would happen, what would that look like?

❖ Have you ever felt that God asked you to do something that you didn't understand? How did you respond?

❖ If you are a mother, have you ever dealt with having a sick child and feeling completely helpless? Other than feeling helpless, how else did you feel?

Chapter 2: Everything I'd Ever Wanted

❖ Have you ever had an experience in your life that you were dead-set against, such as getting married or having children, and then you found that as you aged, you changed your mind? What changed your perspective?

❖ How committed to faith was your family when you were growing up? How did that level of commitment affect your own faith as an adult?

❖ Cyndi felt that her life was perfect. Have you ever had that feeling? What made it that way?

Chapter 3: The Dream

❖ Sometimes God speaks through dreams. Have you ever felt as though God were trying to communicate to you through your dreams? If so, what dream was it? What do you think was his message?

❖ In Cyndi's dream, as she searched frantically, the voice explained to her: "You are looking for the meaning of your life. And your search will lead you straight into the arms of Jesus." In what ways have you searched for meaning? In what ways did it come up short? In what ways did it lead you to Jesus?

Chapter 4: Hiding

❖ Have you ever hidden something from your spouse or a friend? Especially if it was something faith-based? What was it and why did you hide it?

❖ Cyndi wrote that she felt as if she stood at a crossroads. "Do I step out of my comfort zone to get what I want or do I stay comfortable?" Think about a time in your life when you've stood at a crossroads. What was it? What decision did you make? How did that work out?

❖ Cyndi received a vision of standing in front of large crowds and speaking about her faith—something she adamantly refused to do. What has God asked you to do that you were afraid of? Why did you experience fear?

Chapter 5: "It's My Brother's Fault"

❖ How often do you pray? Do you use a rosary or some other method to help you focus? How important is prayer to your life?

❖ Cyndi was afraid of telling her husband the truth about her newfound faith so she told a fib—that her brother was crazy and she needed to go to Medjugorje to watch over him! Think about a time when you lied to cover up something. What was it? How did that lie turn out?

Chapter 6: Signs and Wonders

❖ Have you ever felt that God specifically wanted you to tell him that you love him? Why do you think God wants us to tell him? In what ways does it change us? How often do you tell him of your love for him?

❖ God speaks to us in all sorts of different ways. For Cyndi, she needed to see definite signs. In what ways does God speak to you?

Chapter 7: The Admission

❖ Was there ever a time when you refused to acknowledge God to others—your family, friends, neighbors, coworkers? Why? How did it make you feel afterward?

Chapter 8: The First Night

❖ Have you ever taken a pilgrimage? If so, where? What was that first day like for you? If not, have you ever considered it? Why or why not? Why do you think a pilgrimage may be good for your faith?

❖ In Medjugorje, Mary appeared to teenagers. What do you think the importance of that was?

Chapter 9: Making a Deal with God

❖ Think about a time in which you tried to make a deal with God. What was it over? How did God respond? What happened?

❖ Cyndi promised God that she would live a life that modeled Christ to her family, that she would raise her children to love God, and encourage her husband in his faith. In what ways have you modeled Christ to your family?

Chapter 10: More Signs

❖ Cyndi experienced some rude people who claimed to be Christian and a priest suggested they were rude because they were so excited to get in and pray. Do you believe his statement? Why or why not? In what ways have you seen Christians be rude to one another? How has that made you more aware of how you treat others?

❖ Have you ever experienced a miracle or wonder that you could not explain? What was it? Why do you think some people experience signs and wonders and others don't?

Chapter 11: It's a Girl!

❖ Mother Teresa once said, "In the silence of the heart, God speaks." Do you make time each day to be silent before the Lord? If not, what's keeping you from that? What do you think God could do in your life if you spent some time quietly seeking him?

❖ Cyndi believed that God would never give her children who weren't perfect because she couldn't handle it. Are there things in your life that you've believed you couldn't handle? In what ways did God show you that, through his strength and power, you could handle it?

Chapter 12: Searching for Answers

❖ Sometimes denial is an easy way for us to avoid what we're afraid we may have to face. Think about a time in which you denied the truth of a situation. What was it? What happened that forced you to finally acknowledge the truth?

❖ Searching for answers to a problem can be difficult, straining work—especially when it seems as though no one can help. In what ways have you searched for answers and been disappointed? What was the situation? How did you respond?

Chapter 13: The Diagnosis

❖ No one ever likes to hear bad news. Think about a time in which you received bad news. What was the situation? How did you respond? Think about a time in which you were on the other side and had to give someone else bad news. How did you prepare yourself? How did you feel as you gave the news to the other person? Has it helped you become more compassionate and sensitive to the pain another may bear?

❖ When you receive news, do you prefer to know as many details as possible, or just the basics? Why is that your preference?

Chapter 14: Time to Confess

❖ Confessions are never easy. Think about a time in which you needed to admit something. What was it? To whom did you need to come clean? When you finished, how did the other person respond? How did it feel once you'd confessed?

❖ Have you ever asked others to pray for you or about a specific situation? Have others ever asked you? Did you pray? If not, what kept you from it? Do you think it's important to pray when we tell someone we will? Why or why not?

Chapter 15: Back to Medjugorje

❖ Have you ever prayed for a miracle—or gone to extremes to seek one? What was it? What did you do?

❖ Cyndi realized that rather than pray for her daughter's healing, she needed to pray for God's will to be done. Was she right in that perspective change? Why or why not?

❖ Think about a time when, rather than asking God for something you wanted, you asked him instead for what *he* wanted? How did that feel? What was the outcome? Why do you think it's important to pray that God's will be done rather than our own?

Chapter 16: A Call to Obedience

❖ Why do you think God allows pain in our lives?

❖ Friends offered to keep watch over Cyndi's daughter in the hospital when Cyndi desperately needed rest. That sense of community can be lifesaving. Think about a time in which friends offered to help you. How did that make you feel? Was there ever a time when you were the friend who helped someone? What kind of difference can that type of assistance make in a person's life?

❖ God asked Cyndi to give her rosary to a medical student and Cyndi refused. Has God ever asked you to give up something that was dear to you so that another person could have it? How did you respond? What it the right response? Why or why not? What did you learn from that experience?

Chapter 17: More Desperate Prayers

❖ Thanks to an observant nurse who advised Cyndi to seek professional help, Cyndi was diagnosed with severe depression. Would you take someone's advice to seek help if they offered it? Why or why not?

❖ Cyndi was persistent in her seeking a miracle for her daughter. Do you think God encourages persistence—even if he doesn't respond the way we desire? Why or why not?

❖ Cyndi finally received God's answer: no. Her daughter would not be healed. Think about a time when God didn't answer your prayers in the way you desired. What did you learn about that experience?

Chapter 18: A Tough Surrender

❖ Sometimes God is silent in our pleadings. Why do you think that is? Does that mean that he is not there or not listening?

❖ Cyndi wrestled with God and then finally submitted to his will. Think about a time in which you had to offer a tough surrender. What was it? What happened? In what ways did you grow and learn about yourself? About others? About God?

❖ Again God asked Cyndi to give up something she considered dear—this time it was her crucifix. And this time she said yes. Think about the most recent time you said yes to something God asked you to do. What was it? How did you feel during it? How did you feel afterward? Why do you think God asked that of you at that particular moment?

Chapter 19: Another Child?

❖ Cyndi and her husband, Drew, felt as though God was asking them to have another child. Do you think you could have responded in the same way as they did? Why or why not?

❖ Cyndi wrote: "We look for and expect to find God in the 'whole,' but truly, God is hiding in the 'broken.'" In what ways have you found that to be true in your own life?

❖ Father Sudac had asked the question: "When you die and you go to heaven, and Christ is looking deep into your eyes and asks you, 'Who are you?' What are you going to say?" How would you answer this question?

Chapter 20: The Deepest Pain

❖ Have you lost anyone close to you? What role did that person play in your life? How did that person's death affect your life? In what ways does it continue to affect you?

Chapter 21: The Funeral

❖ Loss is always difficult, but why do you think the loss of a child is the toughest kind of loss?

❖ Cyndi's son Drew Jr. read a passage from the Bible at his sister's funeral. Second Corinthians 4:6-10 (NIV) says,

God, who said, "Let light shine out of darkness," made his light shine in our hearts to give us the light of the knowledge of God's glory displayed in the face of Christ.

But we have this treasure in jars of clay to show that this all-surpassing power is from God and not from us. We are hard pressed on every side, but not crushed; perplexed, but not in despair; persecuted, but not abandoned; struck down, but not destroyed. We always carry around in our body the death of Jesus, so that the life of Jesus may also be revealed in our body.

What does this passage mean to you? In what ways could you apply it to your everyday life?

❖ Cyndi wanted to make people understand that God exists and loves each person very much. Have you ever doubted God's existence? Why? What changed your mentality? In what ways has God shown his love to you this week?

Chapter 22: "We Can Help You"

❖ Do you think abortion is ever a viable option? If so, in what circumstances? If not, why?

❖ Do you think Cyndi made the right decision not to pursue additional testing? Why or why not?

❖ Cyndi had always felt independent and strong, but the death of her daughter made her realize that there are some things we simply cannot control. In what ways have you learned that lesson?

❖ Cyndi's friends tried to encourage her by suggesting that God wouldn't allow the same tragedy to happen again. Why do you think they said that? Do you believe that's true? Why or why not?

Chapter 23: A Healthy Baby Girl

❖ Cyndi said that one of her favorite things with Sarah was simply to change her diapers because Sarah's legs kicked so strongly. Many times it's the simplest things that bring us joy. What small things bring you joy after suffering?

❖ Cyndi believed that Sarah was a gift. Do you believe that something or someone can be a gift, but that God can still remove that from your life? What do you think the purpose would be?

Chapter 24: Blindsided

❖ If you are a parent, you probably have dreams for your children. Have you ever had a dream die—whether for someone you love or for yourself? What was that dream? Why did it die? In what ways have your responded?

❖ Sometimes we think that if we do certain things for God, then he "owes" us something in return. Why is that dangerous thinking?

❖ Have you ever wondered, *What is the point?* when faced with suffering? What did you discover?

❖ Drew wanted Cyndi to be with someone after he gave her the news about their daughter. In what ways can another person offer us comfort? Think of a time when someone was there for you in the midst of your suffering. How did that person help you?

Chapter 25: Return to Medjugorje

❖ When Cyndi went on the retreat with Father Sudac, she initially wasn't going to pray for healing for Sarah, and yet while she was there she began to sense that she should. Do you think she was correct? Why or why not? What would you have done?

❖ Father Sudac said, "All suffering has meaning. Especially the suffering of little children, the holy innocents." Do you agree? In what ways do you think that suffering has meaning? How have you seen that meaning in your own life? What do you think a child's suffering could mean? If that's true, should we not seek a miracle?

Chapter 26: Enjoying Sarah

❖ Cyndi discovered that in her limited time with Sarah, she would choose to enjoy every moment she had left. In what ways do you enjoy your family? Do you take them for granted? How can you change your actions this week to better focus on enjoying and loving those closest to you?

❖ It's natural to want to know the reason for suffering. Do you think it's important? Is "Why, God?" the right question to ask? If so, why? If not, what is a better question?

Chapter 27: Questions for God

❖ Do you believe that God really is all-powerful? How have you lived out that belief? In what ways do you need to trust him more?

❖ Cyndi was angry with God. Do you feel that it's okay to express your anger to God? Think about a time when you were frustrated with him. How did you react? What happened?

❖ What difference does prayer make? Think about a time when God answered a prayer that was important to you—but he answered it in a different way. Did he still answer? What was the outcome? In what ways did it affect your faith?

❖ What are the graces you needed that only could come through bearing a cross of suffering?

Chapter 28: Another Funeral

❖ The apostle Paul wrote in Romans 8:28: "We know that in all things God works for the good of those who love him, who have been called according to his purpose." In what ways have you seen that to be true in your life?

❖ Have you made Jesus the center of your life? What areas are you still holding back from him? Why? What would it take for you to completely give yourself to Jesus?

❖ At the funeral, Cyndi asked the attenders: What is it that we truly want out of life? And how do we make that happen? How would you answer those questions?

❖ Matthew Kelly said: "Tell me your habits, and I'll tell you your life. Tell me your habits, and I'll tell you where your life is going. Tell me your habits, and I'll tell you what you truly value." What would your habits say about your values? Do they lead you toward Christ or away from him?

❖ Mary asks us to do five things in order to grow closer to Jesus: conversion, prayer, reconciliation, Scripture reading, and fasting. In which areas do you need to focus more clearly? When you practice these five things, how have you experienced Christ in a richer and more powerful way?

Chapter 29: A Mother's Vision

❖ Do you think there are some sacrifices only you can make? Why or why not?

Chapter 30: Discovering the Miracles

❖ Looking back over your own suffering, in what ways have you found God to be a faithful companion?

❖ What are you actively doing every day to bring your family closer to Christ? In what areas do you need to be more proactive?

❖ Think about your life. What miracles have you experienced? Did they come the way you might have wanted? How did they draw you closer to God? In what ways have they changed your life? Your relationships? Your faith?

❖ Every person has a cross to bear. Cyndi discovered that God speaks to us through our crosses. In what ways has God reached out to you in the midst of carrying your cross?

APPENDIX B

Medjugorje

Whenever I speak, I inevitably have people ask me about Medjugorje, that mystical place where Mary reportedly appears to the visionaries and where miracles occur every day.

I can only answer that I feel God led me to that place and that's where I grew to trust and understand him better. While I did experience great miracles there, from the miracle of the sun to Nancy's healing, the real miracle was the gift of his love and presence. He never leaves us, never forsakes us, always seeks the best for us, and always loves us. I am a witness to that truth.

Some people question its authenticity. For years the Vatican has looked into the miracles of Medjugorje and some within the church do not believe in its power. But I say, you have to look at the fruit. What becomes of the people who go to Medjugorje? How are they living their lives now? There have been tremendous vocations that have come from people visiting that place. A lot of people have gone into the priesthood and become more devout because of an experience at Medjugorje.

And ministries have been started as a result of a pilgrimage to Medjugorje, such as Rachel's Vineyard, which is a post-abortion healing program. Regardless of whether the miracles are true or not, the fact is that Medjugorje had something to do with the beginnings of those ministries. Whether what they saw was real or fake, I don't know, but something changed their lives.

It radically changed my life. And it's been unswerving.

Through Medjugorje, Mary consistently tries, as any mother would, to point and lead all of her children to true happiness and peace. This can happen only with a life centered on her Son. Mary always points her children to Jesus. Mary has said that all of the miracles in Medjugorje are gifts not from her, but from God. Her messages are meant for people of all faiths and she identifies herself as the "Mother of all people." She asks several things of each person to bring peace in their hearts and God at the center of their lives. They are to (1) pray every day, preferably the rosary; (2) fast on Wednesdays and Fridays (preferably on bread and water); (3) go to confession once a month; (4) read Scripture; and (5) to convert. Conversion is a daily choice for God. It is a commitment and a decision.

Mary says we cannot have peace in the world until we first have peace in our own hearts. We then can bring that peace into our families, then into our communities, and finally into the world. These requests, she says, will bring great peace to the heart of the one who fulfills them. They will take the focus of our lives from that of the world to that of Christ.

The people of Medjugorje live these requests. There is a palpable peace within the town, which serves as an example to the world of what is possible.

For more information about the history and Mary's daily messages, be sure to check out these resources:

Medjugorje: The Message by Wayne Warble. This was the book I first discovered, which then led me to begin my faith search.

Letters from Medjugorje by Wayne Weible

www.medjugorje.hr is the official Medjugorje web site.

www.medjugorje.org is another excellent source of information.

Also, if you're interested in visiting Medjugorje with one of the groups I lead, please contact me at www.cyndipeterson.com .

ACKNOWLEDGMENTS

First and foremost I want to thank my two little girls, Kelly and Sarah. Without them, my life would not contain the depth and richness, peace and joy that I know now. I can never fully express my love for you nor my gratitude for your lives. I cannot wait to see you and hold you both again!

Drew, your love and support throughout the years have been steadfast. I knew you were special the first time I saw you, and you have done nothing but show that to me over and over again. You have an amazing heart, and I love that you chose to share it with me.

To my boys, Drew Jr., Johnny, and Jack, thank you for your constant encouragement and faithfulness. I am so proud to be your mom. You are all amazing young men. Keep your prayer life strong, and remember you have two sisters in heaven praying for you.

To Martha, none of this would have been possible without you. You were always there for me when I needed to talk, someone to cry with, to hug or to laugh with. You knew when to push me and when not to. I am thankful Christ placed you in my life. I pray that everyone can find a friend like you.

To Fr. Donald Timone, thank you for your guidance and patience with me. You are a wealth of wisdom, full of compassion, and delightfully witty. You always made time for me, and I am eternally grateful.

To Fr. Shawn Aaron, I would never have the relationship I do with Christ without you. You taught me discipline, mercy, and the true depths of Christ's love. Thank you for your yes to Christ and for your loyalty to him.

To Msgr. Richard Duncanson, Fr. John Howard, and Sr. Carol Ann Clark, you have been amazing to our family and always there for us.

To Socorro, who has lovingly cared for my children and family. You mean the world to us. Thank you for everything. The girls loved you as if you were their own mother.

To all the teachers, staff, families and students at St. James Academy, your prayers, support, love, dinners and sacrifices made all of this so much easier to bear. You were an amazing part of our journey and we could not have done it without you.

To every nurse, doctor, technician and aide that ever cared for Kelly and Sarah in their time in the Pediatric Intensive Care Unit at Children's Hospital in San Diego, as well as those involved with North County Hospice Care. Your work is beyond amazing. We can never thank you enough for all you did for our girls, and our family. You treated us with dignity and love while providing the best medical care available.

To my agent, Nena Madonia Oshman, for her faithful dedication to completing this book, as well as to everyone at

Salvio Republic including, Emily Hegi, Austin Miller, and Hannah Yancey.

To my outstanding writer, Ginger Kolbaba, who quickly found my voice and placed it in every sentence. You were an answer to prayer, and I am so happy to have found a friend in you as well.

To Steve McEveety, you were so helpful in getting my manuscript into the right hands!

To everyone who ever assisted me in writing this book, especially Ricky McRoskey, your insight, guidance, and professional assistance made this book possible.

And to Wayne Weible, thank you for believing in this book, and helping me along the way.

ABOUT THE AUTHORS

Cynthia Peterson is an accomplished physician, speaker, and mother of five. A board-certified dermatologist, she served for nine years in the US Navy as a flight surgeon and dermatologist. She then entered into private practice after a fellowship specializing in Mohs micrographic surgery. She stopped practicing dermatologic surgery in 2001 after discovering her only daughter had months to live. Since losing her two daughters to Spinal Muscular Atrophy, Cyndi has become a renowned speaker on issues of Medjugorje, life, and the family, and has testified in Washington State against embryonic stem cell research. She has been interviewed by ETWN, Ave Maria radio, and has spoken at numerous national and international conferences to tens of thousands of people. For more information, visit her website at www.cyndipeterson.com.

Ginger Kolbaba is an accomplished, award-winning author, editor, and speaker. She has written or contributed to more than thirty books, including *Your Best Happily Ever After, The Old Fashioned Way*, and *Refined by Fire*. She is a contributing writer for *Thriving Family* magazine and has published more than 400 magazine and online articles for various national and international publications.

Ginger is the former editor of *Today's Christian Woman* and *Marriage Partnership* magazines, both award-winning resources of Christianity Today. She has spoken at national and international conferences, guest lectured at college campuses, and has appeared on national media outlets such as *CNN Headline News* (Nancy Grace), *Court TV*, *Moody Midday Connection*, and *Family Life* radio. She's been quoted in national news outlets such as *Newsweek* and *Chicago Sun-Times*. Visit her at www. gingerkolbaba.com.